# FEELING GUILTY
# FINDING GRACE

If I'm Forgiven, Why Do I Feel So Bad?

## LARRY K. WEEDEN

VINE
BOOKS

SERVANT PUBLICATIONS
ANN ARBOR, MICHIGAN

Vine Books is an imprint of Servant Publications especially designed to serve evangelical Christians.

The names and some of the details of the stories in this book have been changed to protect the privacy of the people involved. Any resemblance to people living or dead is coincidental.

Unless otherwise noted, the Scripture used is from the HOLY BIBLE: NEW INTERNATIONAL VERSION (NIV), © 1973, 1978, 1984 by International Bible Society. Used by permission of Zondervan Publishing House. All rights reserved. Other versions used include: *The Living Bible* (TLB), © 1971 by Tyndale House Publishers, Inc., Wheaton, IL 60189, all rights reserved; *The New Testament in Modern English,* J.B. Phillips Translator, © 1958, 1959, 1960, 1972 J.B. Phillips, used by permission of Macmillan Publishing Company; *The Message: The New Testament in Contemporary Language* by Eugene H. Peterson, © 1993, used by permission of NavPress Publishing Group; the *New King James Version* (NKJV), © 1979, 1980, 1982, 1990, Thomas Nelson Inc., Publishers.

Published by Servant Publications
P.O. Box 8617
Ann Arbor, Michigan 48107

Cover design: Alan Furst

98 99 00  10 9 8 7 6 5 4 3 2 1

Printed in the United States of America
ISBN 1-56955-021-2

LIBRARY OF CONGRESS CATALOGING-IN-PUBLICATION DATA

Weeden, Larry K.
    Feeling guilty, finding grace : if I'm forgiven, why do I feel so bad? / Larry K. Weeden.
        p.   cm.
    Includes bibliographical references.
    ISBN 1-56955-021-2 (alk. paper)
    1. Guilt—Religious aspects—Christianity.   2. Forgiveness of sin.   3. Christian life.   I. Title.
BT722.W44  1998
233'.4—dc21
                                                        98-21986
                                                        CIP

To my wife, Beth,
whose love and support are the epitome of grace;
and to Mom and Dad,
who instilled in me the conviction that God is,
and that He is a rewarder of those who seek Him

# CONTENTS

# FOREWORD

In all the writing and speaking I do, whatever the audience, I make the point that we can find lasting joy only when we seek the fulfillment of every need—emotional, spiritual, and physical—in God. Other people will inevitably let us down. Circumstances can certainly turn against us. Only He loves us perfectly, and only He can be depended upon to always do what's best for us.

But how can we bring ourselves to seek fulfillment in God when, in our heart of hearts, we fear Him—when we feel He's more likely to condemn us than to embrace us?

Sadly, I've found that that's just the way many Christians feel about God. They're wracked by guilt over some past failure or current struggle with a sinful habit. They feel far from Him, and so they experience little joy and no real peace. They know what the Bible says about their sins being forgiven, yet they still feel submerged in a sea of guilt.

What we need is a fresh appreciation of God's mercy and grace. And it needs to be more than just an intellectual understanding. It needs to transform us in that heart of hearts where our thoughts and our actions are born and give direction to our lives. It needs to convince us, perhaps like never before, that we are loved and accepted by God the Father through Jesus His Son.

The book you now hold in your hands, *Feeling Guilty, Finding Grace*, was written to help you gain that greater appreciation of God's goodness. The author, whom I've known and enjoyed working with for more than ten years now, has had his own struggles with guilt and found new depths in God's grace. I believe the time you spend with him in these pages will be one of the best investments you could make in yourself and in your relationship with God and others.

This a book of hope. It's a book of joy. Its message, if you let it sink into the core of your being, will have you thanking and praising God and, if you're like me, feeling closer to Him than ever before.

Read this book prayerfully. Share it with others who also need it. You and they will be very glad you did.

Gary Smalley
Branson, Missouri
April 1998

# ACKNOWLEDGMENTS

For whatever help this book provides to God's people, I have to thank many people:

My parents reared me to know that God is, that He loves us, and that the Bible is His Word.

My wife, Beth, shows me God's love and patience every day—and also gives me a swift kick in the pants when I need it.

My son, Matthew, continually brings me joy and helps to keep me humble.

An early Sunday school teacher named Norrie Polhill loved the boys in his class and kick-started my love for the written word.

Gwen Ellis and Bert Ghezzi at Servant Publications believed in this project enough to give it a chance at life on the printed page.

My friend and former pastor Steve Thurman impressed upon me indelibly the awesome wonder of God's relentless grace. He and my friend and colleague Al Janssen, among others, read the draft version of this book and offered valuable feedback.

My editors, Liz Heaney and Deena Davis, helped me to polish my words and thoughts and make this a better book than it would have been otherwise.

My friend Gary Smalley graciously encouraged me in my

writing efforts and agreed to lend his support by writing the foreword to this book.

Most of all, I thank my Lord and Savior, Jesus Christ, for extending His grace to me. He gives purpose to my life and hope that my meager work will in some way be used for His glory.

For whatever is of value in the following pages, I have to thank these and other people too numerous to mention. For whatever is lacking or misleading, I alone am at fault. And for whatever is praiseworthy, may God alone be praised.

# It Happened Years Ago

Most folks, it seems, are better acquainted with their
guilt and shame than with their God.

CHARLES SWINDOLL[1]

He doesn't even remember the incident, but I'm sure I'll
never forget it. I'm not sure if I'll ever be able to forgive
myself.

My son was only six or seven at the time, and he was, as
they say, a strong-willed child. His stubbornness showed up
especially at bedtime, as with so many kids. I didn't know how
to handle him or my emotions.

I've forgotten most of the details of that night, for which
I'm grateful. What I do remember is that he was being unco-
operative, it was well past his regular bedtime, and I was getting
more and more exasperated. Was he being willfully defiant, seeing how far he could push me? Maybe. Probably. But that was
no excuse for what I did.

The end to that evening is a scene forever burned into my
memory. He still wasn't ready for bed, standing there in his
room in his underwear, and I finally reached the end of my self-
control. All my badgering, threatening, and whatever else I

tried had failed. I completely lost my temper and began yelling at him at the top of my voice. My anger carried me away, and I went on and on about how mad I was, how he didn't listen, how fed up I was.

In a perverse sort of way, it felt good. By the time I was done, my throat was sore.

And through it all, my son stood there, shaking and screaming in terror.

God help me, but the boy I love more than life itself was scared to death of the raving madman I became in those few minutes. The son whose love and respect I crave had only fear in his eyes that night.

Finally, I got some control of myself, growled (literally), and stalked out of the room. Over the years, putting Matthew to bed at night has been a highlight of my days, but that night I wanted nothing more to do with him. I was afraid of losing it again. It was left to his mother to console him.

I'm glad mothers are there to do such things, and I'm glad that as young boys grow up, they don't remember every unpleasant thing that has happened to them. But as I said before, I doubt I'll ever forget it. I tried to justify my behavior, to convince myself that it was his fault I had lost control, but I couldn't buy it then and I certainly don't now. My anger soon gave way to self-loathing. *What kind of father am I?* I wondered. *What kind of man am I? What kind of Christian am I? How can I say I love him and then turn into a monster that has him quivering in fear?*

That night had lasting consequences. I felt so terrible—so guilty—that I promised myself I would never again raise my voice to him that way. I've kept that promise, and in the process I've gone to the other extreme and probably been too lenient a disciplinarian. I suppose I'll never be qualified to write a parenting book. But I don't regret making and keeping that promise.

Today my son is fifteen, and he and I are fast friends. Besides that, he's a pretty good kid if I do say so myself, so maybe I (and my wife, of course) have done something right after all.

Why do I tell that story? Perhaps you can relate, or perhaps you feel you've done something far worse. But it's a good example of a common experience, one I'd guess you share since you're reading this book. I did something wrong. It made me feel terribly guilty. I prayed that night and asked God to forgive me. I've prayed the same prayer many more times since.

In my mind, from what I believe about the Bible, God, and my relationship with Him, I know I'm forgiven. But even though the incident happened years ago, and even though my mind tells me I'm already completely forgiven, my heart still isn't sure. And I'm still not completely at peace about it. I still feel guilty (I did something wrong and deserve to be punished) and ashamed (therefore, I must not be a very good person—certainly not a very good parent).

Why is that? If the Bible says I'm forgiven—if I believe God loves and accepts me and has removed my sin from me as far as the east is from the west—why do I still feel guilty and disgraced about that night? Why, every time I remember that night, do I cringe inwardly and think once again that I must have been a lousy father, a complete failure at one of the most important responsibilities God will ever give me? Why is the pain of that memory still so strong? And why am I tempted to conclude that because of what I did that night, God can't love and accept me completely?

I've thought long and hard about that, and I think God has given me some insight into the problem. It *is* a problem, because I don't think God wants any of us who claim His Son as our Savior to feel guilty when He has already extended forgiveness.

I'm still on that journey of discovery, and I invite you to come with me. The end of the line is in heaven, but there's a lot to learn along the way. I pray that the truths I've learned will be a help and a comfort to you.

But maybe you're thinking you have done something far worse, and you're wondering if this book will apply to your guilt. Perhaps you've had an extramarital relationship or even committed adultery. Well, as Jesus defined adultery in the Sermon on the Mount (an act of desire as much as it is a physical act), I've done that, too. You might have gone so far as to kill someone; by Jesus' standard, I've violated that law of God as well. While your and my specific offenses may differ, the lasting feelings of guilt with which we struggle—their causes, their effects in our lives, and their "cures"—are the same. So please keep reading and see if you can't find nourishment for your soul.

Here's one more lasting consequence of that time when I screamed at my son: For years I've lived with the memory of how horrible I was that night, but not until my wife read these pages for the first time was I reminded that I did do something right that evening. "You went in and apologized to him later," she said. "You couldn't let him go to sleep without hearing your apology."

So I did one good thing. I might get to write that parenting book after all. But isn't it interesting that over the years I have vividly remembered the wrong I did but had entirely forgotten the good.

That's part of the nature of guilt. It's a powerful emotion. I've found that the only thing more powerful is the grace of God. That sounds like a cliché, but it's not. It is, in fact, life's most profound truth.

# God's Truth About Our Guilt

For twenty centuries the Church has been proclaiming
salvation, and the grace and forgiveness of God, to a
humanity oppressed with guilt. How then is it that even
amongst the most fervent believers there are so few
free, joyous, confident souls?

PAUL TOURNIER[1]

Susan is a Christian woman. She has been married to Stan
for almost twenty years, and to most observers they've had
a normal, fairly healthy marriage. But appearances can be
deceiving.

At the time I'm writing this, they're in the process of getting
a divorce. Why?

Before they were married, Susan and Stan engaged in a sexual relationship. She knew it was wrong at the time, and she
confessed her sin to God. She also thought that somehow,
marrying Stan would make everything all right. It didn't.

Despite praying about it many times over the years, Susan
has never been able to shake the feeling of guilt and shame
about what she and Stan did that long time ago. She feels
soiled and dirty. She doubts that God has ever really forgiven

her and so fears Him; she certainly hasn't forgiven herself. Nor has she ever completely forgiven Stan.

This nagging guilt, lack of forgiveness, and doubting of God's love combined to form an acid that ate away at their marriage. Slowly but steadily, it dissolved whatever warmth and affection they had enjoyed in the beginning. "I was foolish to think I could escape the consequences of what we did," Susan concludes.

Now their relationship stands on the brink of destruction.

Like Susan, many Christians I talked to about this book, when I first told them the subject, immediately had some incident in their lives come to mind—something they did in the past that haunts them with guilt even today. Others said that while no one specific incident stood out in their memory, they still felt guilty much of the time and didn't experience much of the "joy of the Lord."

At the time I'm writing this, I've been a Christian for thirty-five years. I was raised in a Christian home by good, godly, and loving parents. Yet I still often feel guilty about things I've already confessed to God. It's still easy to feel alienated from Him, and I'm frequently tempted to try to hide from Him rather than seek His embrace. It still seems more natural to feel condemned and unworthy rather than pardoned and beloved of God.

Jesus said, "I have come that [My people] may have life, and have it to the full" (Jn 10:10). So why do many of us seem so often to have souls constricted by guilt rather than overflowing with God's grace?

It's not as if we don't know the scriptures that speak of God's love and forgiveness. There are, for instance, the familiar words of Romans 8:1: "Therefore, there is now no condemnation for those who are in Christ Jesus." That statement by the apostle Paul is one of the great truths of the Bible. Christians through the centuries, right up until today, have believed it. If we have trusted in Jesus as our Savior, God has declared us forgiven of even the most heinous sins and removed them an immeasurably great distance from us.

*In our everyday experience, however, many of us live as though it were not true because we don't* feel *forgiven.*

In fact, we feel guilty, judged, afraid, and condemned—by ourselves, by other Christians, and by God Himself. We feel that we've done unforgivable things. We feel we've failed as Christians so often that God must have run out of patience with us long ago. We feel that if others knew what we're really like, they would be appalled and would reject us completely. Our sense of guilt is so great that it has turned to shame; we've done and still do so many bad things that we must be bad people—certainly bad Christians. Besides, we're supposed to feel guilty, aren't we?

We're like the people described by pastor and professor David Seamands: "Again and again Christians tell me, 'I feel guilty almost all the time.' When I ask, 'Aren't there times when you don't feel guilty, or when you have a sense of being at peace with God?' they often answer, 'Not really, because then I feel guilty for not feeling guilty!'"[2]

Even the most wise and biblically knowledgeable among us—people who seem to "have it all together" spiritually—can struggle with feelings of guilt. Their years of Christian experience are no guarantee of freedom, joy, and confidence in the Lord.

Consider the case of C.S. Lewis, one of the great Christian thinkers of this or any age. Gifted with rare intellect, he became a university professor and prolific author. After periods as an atheist and then a theist, he finally became a Christian at the age of thirty-three in 1931. He published his first Christian book just two years later, and he went on to write such classics as the Narnia Chronicles and *Mere Christianity*, among others.

To say Lewis had a profound understanding of God, the Bible, and the Christian faith would be a major understatement. Yet look at what he wrote in a letter dated December 26, 1951—*twenty years after his conversion:*

> During the past year a great joy has befallen me.... It is astonishing that sometimes we believe that we believe what, really, in our heart, we do not believe.
>
> For a long time I believed that I believed in the forgiveness of sins. But suddenly ... this truth appeared in my mind in so clear a light that I perceived that never before ... had I believed it with my whole heart.
>
> So great is the difference between mere affirmation by the intellect and that faith, fixed in the very marrow and as it were palpable, which the Apostle wrote was *substance*.[3]

Even Lewis, for all his intellect and understanding, apparently had not taken God's forgiveness to heart in almost twenty years of Christian living. His head knowledge of biblical truth had not translated into freedom from feelings of guilt. And the same is true for many of us as well.

## What the Bible Tells Us

Perhaps if Romans 8:1 stood alone in the whole Bible, it would be easier to understand why we often struggle to feel forgiven.

But far from standing by itself, it's only one of many verses that speak of God's grace. Here are just a few familiar passages of Scripture that echo that same message loud and clear:

Who will bring any charge against those whom God has chosen? It is God who justifies. Who is he that condemns? Christ Jesus, who died—more than that, who was raised to life—is at the right hand of God and is also interceding for us. Who shall separate us from the love of Christ?

ROMANS 8:33-35

For God was in Christ,... no longer counting men's sins against them but blotting them out. This is the wonderful message.

2 CORINTHIANS 5:19, TLB

Christ died for the ungodly.... Since we have now been justified by his blood, how much more shall we be saved from God's wrath through him! ... Not only is this so, but we also rejoice in God through our Lord Jesus Christ, through whom we have now received reconciliation.

ROMANS 5:6, 9, 11

For Christ died for sins once for all, the righteous for the unrighteous, to bring you to God.

1 PETER 3:18

If we confess our sins, he is faithful and just and will forgive us our sins and purify us from all unrighteousness.

1 JOHN 1:9

He does not treat us as our sins deserve or repay us according to our iniquities. For as high as the heavens are above the earth, so great is his love for those who fear him; as far as the east is from the west, so far has he removed our transgressions from us.

PSALM 103:10-12

But you were washed, you were sanctified, you were justified in the name of the Lord Jesus Christ and by the Spirit of our God.

1 CORINTHIANS 6:11

But you are a chosen people, a royal priesthood ... that you may declare the praises of him who called you out of darkness into his wonderful light.... Once you had not received mercy, but now you have received mercy.

1 PETER 2:9-10

I leave behind with you—peace; I give you my own peace and my gift is nothing like the peace of this world. You must not be distressed and you must not be daunted.

JOHN 14:27-28, PHILLIPS

As far as God is concerned there is a sweet, wholesome fragrance in our lives. It is the fragrance of Christ within us, an aroma to both the saved and the unsaved all around us.

2 CORINTHIANS 2:15, TLB

For being saved is a gift; if a person could earn it by being good, then it wouldn't be free—but it is! It is given to those who do not work for it. For God declares sinners to be good in his sight if they have faith in Christ to save them from God's wrath. King David spoke of this, describing the happiness of an undeserving sinner who is declared "not guilty" by God. "Blessed, and to be envied," he said, "are those whose sins are forgiven and put out of sight. Yes, what joy there is for anyone whose sins are no longer counted against him by the Lord."

ROMANS 4:4-8, TLB

I could go on and on quoting verses in the same vein. They all declare that our guilt has been removed for all time and we are forgiven for every sin we've ever committed or ever will; that we have been made right with God and have peace with Him; that we are acceptable and even pleasing to Him, imperfect as we still are; and that we are His people, and no one can bring a charge against us.

As Bible-believing Christians, we claim to embrace those statements as the unfailing, infallible truth of God. That, indeed, is what they are. Perhaps, for a fortunate few of you who read this, simply being reminded of them here will be enough to give you an experience of joy similar to that about which C.S. Lewis wrote.

Yet somehow, for most of us, the truth that we accept at a theological and intellectual level—that we are forgiven of *all* sin and have been declared not guilty by God for all time—rarely finds its way into our hearts and the conduct of our daily lives.

## How We Respond

Peter wrote in the passage quoted above that we are God's priests; the Lord has invited us into His royal throne room to praise Him, consult with Him, and be comforted by Him.

Further, the writer to the Hebrews encouraged us to approach His throne of grace with confidence (see Heb 4:16). But when I think about our difficulty in accepting grace and feeling forgiven, I imagine a scene something like this:

We have our invitation to enter God's presence, yet we refuse. It's as if we stand outside, hanging our heads in fear and shame. So an angel comes out to ask why we don't accept God's welcome, and we try to hide behind the drapes or the potted plants. When he pulls us into the open, we protest, "You don't know what I've done! I'm not good enough to enter God's presence! He'll condemn me!"

Shaking his head, the angel goes back into the throne room. We breathe a sigh of relief.

Before long, however, out comes Abraham to talk with us. "Do you remember," he says, "how I lied about my wife and almost caused her to commit adultery, not once but twice? And how I jumped the gun on God's plan and tried to create in my own way the child He had promised? Yet God extended mercy to me and even held me up before the whole world as a model of faith! So why don't you join me in the throne room? God wants to take you into His arms and tell you how much He loves you."

But we say instantly, "No, I can't."

Abraham shakes his head sadly and walks back in.

A few minutes go by, and here comes Moses. "Don't you know that I murdered a man," he asks, "and that on several key occasions I deliberately disobeyed God, even though I had seen Him as no other man has? Yet the Lord loved me and used me in a great way to lead His people and even write part of His holy Scripture. Why don't you come in with me and let Him love you in the same way?"

But we insist, "You don't know all the things I've done! I couldn't possibly."

Moses sighs heavily and goes back to God without us.

Next we're visited by Jonah, who explains how he turned his back on God and ran but was pursued nonetheless by His relentless love. Then comes David, who confesses to adultery and murder, with negligent parenting thrown in on the side, but who in spite of all that, by God's grace, came to be known as a man after the Lord's own heart.

"Come in," each of them says. "The heavenly Father wants to show His mercy to you as well."

But we will not.

Finally, Jesus Himself walks out to extend His personal invitation. "Think of all I accomplished for you on the cross," He pleads. "Haven't you seen My truths in your Bible?"

"But I don't *feel* forgiven!" we each insist. And there we stand, as if cemented to the floor.

That scenario might strike some as far-fetched, yet it illustrates the practical effect of our response to God's grace—we have an incredible capacity to live as if the truth were not true. And it captures the dominant role our emotions play in our relationship with Him, just as they do in every other area of our lives.

In the case of that awful night described in chapter one, for example, when I screamed at my son and ended up feeling like the worst father in the world, I have struggled ever since to feel completely forgiven. In my heart of hearts, it's as if I'm still saying to God a decade later, "Yeah, I know You've forgiven me and he's forgiven me, but we all realize that incident revealed just how bad a dad I really am. And there's no way my guilt over that can ever be entirely erased."

In that "heart of hearts" part of my being, then, I have yet to reconcile completely what I know biblically with what I feel.

## Where We're Going

In part one of this book, beginning with the next chapter, we'll look at some of the reasons behind our difficulty in feeling in our hearts what our heads know to be true—things like the fickleness of feelings, the legalism rampant among Christians, our lack of experience with unconditional love, and the wearing effect of habitual sin. We'll also examine Satan's role in the matter. And then in part two, we'll consider how our emotions might be brought into closer alignment with the truths of Scripture.

My goal is *not* to add to anyone's guilt with the thought that you're somehow making God out to be a liar if you don't feel forgiven. Rather, I want to offer hope that the things you understand intellectually and theologically can take root more and more in the very core of your being.

*The abundant life offered by Jesus in John 10:10 can be ours.*

---

# part one

# Why We Struggle
# to Feel Forgiven

# When Our Feelings Get in the Way

I wrote a book years ago called *Emotions: Can You Trust Them?* and spent about 200 pages saying 'no.'

JAMES DOBSON[1]

D an is the sole pastor of a modest-sized church in a small town. He loves his work and definitely feels called to it by God. His parishioners enjoy his sermons and trust his advice. Between preparing messages, meeting with various church boards, performing weddings and funerals, and counseling with couples and families, he routinely puts in sixty- to seventy-hour work weeks. Everything is going great … except for just one problem.

Dan and his wife have three young sons. Because his work takes up so much of his time and energy, he has little of either left for them (or his wife). They're essentially growing up without a father.

Every time Dan thinks about the situation, he feels guilty. He knows he's doing a poor job as a father, failing day after day in the biblical admonition to "train a child in the way he should go" (Prv 22:6). Yet he doesn't see how he can make any more time available for them. So even though the church is going well, Dan has a nagging feeling that he's really a failure in God's eyes.

Tiffany is a Christian teenage girl who attends a public high school. In this day and age, that means she's constantly bombarded with foul language. Her friends and other class-mates use profanity routinely in casual conversation, not seeming to give it a second thought. Even some teachers think nothing of sprinkling their lectures with obscenities.

Now the habit is rubbing off on Tiffany. She finds herself, against her wishes, swearing with her friends from time to time.

As soon as the words are out of her mouth, she always feels convicted and guilty. She knows there's a Bible verse she's violating that says we should only speak words that build oth-ers up. When she uses the Lord's name, she realizes, she's even breaking one of the Ten Commandments.

Every time this happens, Tiffany tries to pray for forgive-ness. Yet she feels uncomfortable about it, because she has done it so many times before and keeps on doing it. *Surely God is getting fed up with me by now,* she figures. And more and more, she feels far from God. Compared to just a year ago, she's reading her Bible less, praying less, and feeling less desire to go to church and youth group.

A baby girl was born with spina bifida, a congenital condi-tion that creates a hole in the spinal column, and her mother felt guilty. Why? "I thought I was being punished because I had quit going to church," she says. Her husband was a faith-ful church attendee, so she figured the "responsibility" for their child's condition must all be hers. "Every time we would face some new problem, I'd start crying and say, 'I know God is punishing me.'"[2]

In a different yet related vein, I confess that I'm addicted to sports on TV. I can sit down to watch a football or baseball game, and then the game that follows, and then the golf or tennis tournament that comes on, and before I know it I've blown an entire Saturday.

When I get to the end of such a day and reflect on how I spent my time, I feel a deep sense of guilt. I feel as though I've disrespected God's gifts of time and energy—of life. Further, I feel that I've wasted the opportunity to be out doing something—anything—good rather than letting myself be "entertained to death."

It doesn't matter how hard or long I've worked the week before or how tired I am. Nor does it seem to matter whether I ask God to forgive me; I still tend to feel like a lazy slug and a poor specimen of a Christian.

The people covered by these illustrations—and all of you who can relate to one or more of our struggles—have at least three things in common. First, we live with a continual sense of feeling guilty to one degree or another. Second, since we *feel* guilty, we tend to conclude that we must, in fact, *be* guilty. And third, we easily conclude, based on our feelings, that because of the nature of what we've done or how often we've done it, we're somehow loved less by God than other Christians.

## Children of Our Age

We are, in that way, typical children of our age. Our lives—our thoughts, our daily choices, and even our life-changing decisions—are controlled by our feelings. Thus, while one of our credos is "If I feel guilty, I am guilty," the opposite side of the coin, which we also embrace, is "If it feels good, do it, because it must *be* good."

The McDonald's company captured this spirit perfectly in its ad campaign that said simply, "You deserve a break today." It appealed to our natural desire to feel good. *I've been working hard*, the rationale goes. *I'm tired and I'm hungry.* So we decide to let a fast-food restaurant do our cooking. Never mind the high cost compared to eating at home, the high fat content, and the lack of nutrition in a bag of french fries. The meal tastes good and offers instant gratification. It has become the modern way to "cook."

Is this decision wise? Is it in my long-term best interests? Is it consistent with my most deeply held values? Have I considered all the alternatives and assessed the situation correctly? These questions are frequently ignored today. In their place, we ask only one: What do I feel like doing?

Recently, I made a major decision in exactly this way. My wife and I badly needed to replace our car. It was worn out, leaking oil, and unreliable despite constant transfusions of new cash. For a long time we put up with it because we simply couldn't afford to buy another. But finally we got the money together to get a decent used car without going into debt.

Before we went car shopping, I cautioned my wife, "Let's not rush into anything. We don't want to grab the first thing we see that we like; we want to check out at least five or six dealerships. And for sure we don't want to get emotional and gush over a car, because then we'll lose whatever bargaining power we might have with the salesman."

She agreed that was the wise approach and said she would try to contain her enthusiasm for any car she saw that she really liked.

To her credit, she stuck with that strategy.

To my credit, I lasted through one dealership.

The first place we went, the salesman showed us a car that probably would have met our needs. It had ample rear seat room for our long-legged son, adequate power, and even some nice extras. But I managed to say—even after the salesman warned that such a fine car wouldn't last long (a standard salesman's line, I'm sure)—"We're just starting to look, and we need to visit a few more dealerships before making a decision."

I was proud of my self-restraint as we drove off to the next place on our list.

At the second dealership, I remained objective and businesslike as the sales rep showed us first one car and then another. Then he said, "I don't know if you'll be interested, but we've got these other cars that are such a good deal that I like to show them to people." And he led us to a set of cars, different versions of the same model, that made me start drooling.

I had studied this model in magazines and ads. It looked good and had more than enough room and power, but I had dismissed it from consideration because I didn't think there was any way we would ever be able to afford one. Now here I was, looking at a handful of these cars, any of which could be ours.

Of course, even used these cars cost more than we had to spend, but I immediately started to rationalize, *What's a few thousand dollars of debt when you have a chance to get a car like this? We can handle it. We'll probably even be able to pay it off early.*

When I got behind the wheel for a test drive, with the salesman in the backseat, I knew I wanted one of these cars. As I played with the cruise control, I said, "Neat!" As I adjusted the power outside mirrors, I said, "This is really nice!" As I accelerated onto the freeway with ease, I smiled and said, "Plenty of power!"

My wife sat next to me, and I could just imagine her thinking, *Who said we shouldn't let on how much we like a car?* And then her facial expression told me she must be thinking, *I guess we're getting one of these cars.* And indeed, I had already made up my mind.

Now, I can give you a number of valid reasons why the car we bought is a good car for us. We do enjoy it. But it *doesn't* make financial sense to borrow money for a car, which I knew. The simple fact is that when I saw the car and realized the price was at least close to what we had to spend, my reasoning shut down and my emotions took over. I wanted that car, I was excited by that car, and that was all that mattered in a decision involving what is, for us, a lot of money. No more objectivity. No more analysis of options. I was operating purely on feelings.

Psychologist Dr. James Dobson, in his book *Emotions: Can You Trust Them?* put the situation in our culture (and in my car-buying decision) this way: "Emotional experience in the western world has become *the* primary motivation of values and actions and even spiritual beliefs. Furthermore (and this is the point), we are living in a day when people are being encouraged to release their emotions, to grant them even greater power in ruling their destinies.... We live and breathe by the vicissitudes of our feelings.... Reason is now dominated by feelings, rather than the reverse as God intended."[3]

Peter Steele, from the heavy metal band Type O Negative, described our society more bluntly when he declared, "The best term for what we do is 'gland rock.' I think that most people are pretty much governed by their hormones, and so are we."[4]

## The Problem With Feelings

The problem with living by our feelings, including judging how guilty we *are* by how guilty we *feel*, is that our feelings are often a poor barometer of reality. It's easy to feel guilty when, by a biblical standard, we don't need to. Yet we continue to give our feelings more credence than they deserve.

The simple fact is that our emotions fluctuate all the time. We can go to church and have a wonderful worship experience, feel close to God, and bask in the assurance of His forgiveness. But ten minutes later, in the car, the kids start acting up, we start getting upset and saying things we shouldn't, and all of a sudden we're condemning ourselves again for our inability to control our temper.

How many times have you been in a situation that at the time made you feel terribly upset, yet when it was over, you realized, *That wasn't so bad after all?* How often have you enjoyed an event (a movie, for example) or laughed at a joke and later had to conclude it was superficial or silly or even insulting? The feelings of the moment can be so misleading.

Our emotions during the course of a given day or week might be compared to riding on a roller coaster. For brief periods (longer for some than for others), if we're in our normal routine, we might be on a fairly level stretch. At times, when things are going well or we're doing something enjoyable, it's as if we're climbing into the sky and enjoying the view, taking in the whole amusement park and feeling good. But at other times, when life takes a turn for the worse, our emotions take a correspondingly wild plunge down into fear, anger, doubt, or bitterness.

As our feelings fluctuate, our sense of relationship with God—of where we stand with Him—often fluctuates right along with them. Is this any way to assess our guilt or innocence before a holy God? No, it's not.

## The Source of Our Guilty Feelings

Many Christians, if not most, are constantly weighed down with guilty feelings. In spite of our understanding of God's forgiveness, we can't escape them. We find ourselves thinking and acting and even assessing our self-worth based on them. All this raises the question: Where do these feelings come from? What are the sources of these feelings that plague our existence day in and day out, robbing us of the abundant life Jesus intends for us to experience?

Of course, there are times when we as Christians *ought* to feel guilty—not condemned, because Jesus paid the price for all our sins—when we've violated one of His standards (i.e., sinned) and we haven't yet confessed it or made amends with someone we wronged in the process. That's genuine guilt, produced by the indwelling Holy Spirit, that is meant to drive us back into God's loving, forgiving arms.

But so often, our guilty feelings are of a different character. We feel guilty not because we violated a biblical command but because we violated a cultural, family, or personal rule, either explicit or unspoken. The violation of these rules is *false* guilt. Yet the feelings of inadequacy and unworthiness that it engenders can be even stronger than those brought on by genuine guilt, because in this case the "offense" is against someone we can touch and talk to, and in whose eyes we can see the disappointment.

A wife and mother who works outside the home, for instance, may feel guilty simply because she doesn't make her family homemade bread every week. Why the guilt? Her own mother, who was a full-time homemaker, always baked fresh bread for her family, and without saying a word about it, she passed that expectation—that family rule about what moms do for their families—to her daughter. Now the grown daughter lacks the time and energy to do the same for her own husband and kids, but no matter, she feels guilty because she hasn't lived up to her mother's example. She also feels a sense of God's disapproval because she's not a "Proverbs 31 woman," seemingly able to "do it all."

Then there's the kind of guilt I experience relative to that traumatic incident with my young son (recounted in chapter one). We did something wrong in the past, perhaps years ago. We confessed it to God. We asked for forgiveness from those we hurt, and we made amends. Yet despite having done those things, we still feel guilty. We may have confessed it and asked for God's cleansing over and over, literally hundreds of times in some cases. We may have gone way overboard in trying to "make it up" to the person we offended. But we just can't shake the guilty feeling.

*This, too, is false guilt.* (The root source here is Satan, "the accuser" [Rv 12:10], which we'll cover more fully in chapter eight.)

Another source of guilt is the general existence of sin in our world. We read the newspaper or see the television news and understand that crime, injustice, and suffering are rampant in the world. And unless we're totally unfeeling, we can't help but experience a vague sense of guilt about being better off. Or we feel that we're somehow expected to improve things—to put an end to hunger or racism or totalitarian governments—though we usually don't know how.[5]

Guilt also arises from the harm we cause others, even unintentionally. Professor Lewis Smedes points out, concerning this kind of guilt, "The more decent we are the more acutely we feel our pain for the unfair hurts we caused. Our pain becomes our hate. The pain we cause other people becomes the hate we feel for ourselves.... We judge, we convict, and we sentence ourselves."[6] Perhaps you can relate to this one.

Still another source of guilt is the failure to live up to our own expectations, especially in an area that's important to us. For example, when my wife tells me we don't have enough money in the checking account to pay all our bills in a given month (fortunately, it hasn't happened too often), I feel a twinge of guilt, because I've accepted the role of primary breadwinner for our family. It's one of my chief responsibilities. Her news makes me feel as though I've failed in that duty.

Psychiatrist Paul Tournier also pointed out that we all experience guilt over life's inevitable conflicts with others: "All life brings conflict.... Thus we have only the choice between several guilts: guilt from asserting ourselves or guilt from being silent.... There is no life without conflict; no conflict without guilt."[7]

Then there's the guilt we feel because we struggle constantly with habitual sin in one or more areas of our lives. Greed and materialism; the desire for power and control; lust; laziness; a caustic tongue; hatred; drunkenness—these are just some of the common sins that master us all too easily, bathing us in guilt each time we succumb.

The apostle Paul, in one of the Bible's better-known passages, captured the feeling of every person who struggles with habitual sin: "I do not understand what I do. For what I want to do I do not do, but what I hate I do.... I know that nothing good lives in me, that is, in my sinful nature. For I have the desire to do what is good, but I cannot carry it out. For what I do is not the good I want to do; no, the evil I do not want to do—this I keep on doing" (Rom 7:15, 18-19).

Indeed, we tend to commit the same sin over and over to the point that we conclude the situation is hopeless and we'll never get that habit "under control." (We'll look more closely at our feelings related to habitual sin in chapter six.)

We also tend to conclude that God *must* have run out of patience and forgiveness for that area of our lives long ago. In that sense, while we may be able to quote orthodox doctrine about biblical forgiveness, our practical theology of God is badly off base and even pagan—that is, it's like every other religion in the world in that it assumes we have to somehow earn God's favor.

I'll say much more about this later, but for now I would observe that the principal emotion toward God that's involved in this mind-set is not joy or peace or affection but rather fear. As writer Philip Yancey has observed in contrasting Christianity with other faiths, "Hindus offer sacrifices at the temple. Kneeling Muslims bow down so low that their foreheads touch the ground. In most religious traditions, in fact, *fear* is the primary emotion when one approaches God."[8]

Unfortunately, that's also true of many Christians. Pastor Dan, for example, whose story was told at the beginning of this chapter, fears God as the One who will judge him for his failures as a father in spite of all the work he has done for his church. Tiffany, the teenager prone to profanity, fears God will condemn her for misusing His name so easily; that's why she distances herself from Him.

Yancey goes on to offer an illustration of how we often—in practical, everyday terms—relate to God. Yancey used to keep a saltwater aquarium, which proved to be a demanding assignment. He had to keep the water clean with two different kinds of filters, and he had to pump in enzymes, vitamins, and antibiotics regularly. Of course, he also had to feed the fish three times a day. Altogether, it required a major commitment on his part.

How did the fish respond? Were they grateful? Loving? No. Regardless of how much Yancey did for them, day after day, their response every time he came near the tank was fear. He was simply too big and too foreboding for them, his kind actions on their behalf totally beyond their understanding. Because they didn't know him and he was so big in their eyes, they perceived him only as a threat, a potential enemy.

Likewise we, not really knowing God and His character, tend to see Him as huge, foreboding, and beyond human comprehension. We fear Him more than we love Him. Rather than reveling in His grace and mercy, we expect Him to stomp on us at any moment in vindictive judgment.

Yet another reason we feel guilty is that we know instinctively that everything has to be paid for, especially every sin. Dr. Tournier wrote of this, "The notion that everything has to be paid for is very deep-seated and active within us, as universal as it is unshakable by logical argument. So the very people who long most ardently for grace have the greatest difficulty in accepting it. It would be too simple a solution, and a kind of intuition opposes it."[9]

In other words, we realize, as the Bible says, that "without the shedding of blood there is no forgiveness" (Heb 9:22). What we have trouble accepting, at the emotional level anyway, is that "the death he [Jesus] died, he died to sin once for all" (Rom 6:10) and "Therefore, there is now no condemnation for those who are in Christ Jesus" (Rom 8:1). We feel that somehow, in some way, despite the logical impossibility of it, we still have to atone for our own sins.

I'm reminded of the truism that says, "When you have a hammer in your hand, everything looks like a nail." In the same way, when we're convinced we're still guilty and standing under God's judgment, we tend to find in the Bible those verses that reinforce our opinion. We're drawn, for instance, to verses like Romans 3:23 ("For all have sinned and fall short of the glory of God") and Isaiah 53:6 ("We all, like sheep, have gone astray, each of us has turned to his own way").

We see what we expect to see and little, if anything, else. (Academics call this "confirmation bias.") And what we see confirms our feeling of being hopelessly condemned.

## Making Sense of Our Feelings

If our feelings exert such a powerful influence on us, growing out of so many deep-rooted sources, yet they're unreliable indicators of our true state of guilt or innocence, how do we make sense of them? How do we get and keep them in proper perspective so that we can translate what we know theologically of God's grace into a true and abiding appreciation of that grace that fosters a closer and more loving relationship with Him?

Part of the answer is to understand where our guilty feelings are coming from, which is the purpose of this chapter and the rest of this section. Another part will be found in the next section of the book, where we'll look in depth at the "cure" for guilty feelings that don't stand up to biblical scrutiny.

But for now, let me pass along a practical way I have discovered to test the validity of guilty feelings. It comes from Dr. James Dobson, in his book *Emotions: Can You Trust Them?* It involves looking as objectively as we can at three things. We examine our emotions by asking, What do I feel? We examine our intellect by asking, Is the feeling reasonable or biblical? And we examine our will by asking, What was my intent?

If we're truly guilty, Dobson says, the answers to all three questions should point to guilt. If even one response points to innocence—if, for example, we can honestly say we did not make a deliberate choice to sin in the thing about which we feel guilty—then the feeling is not valid.[10]

Let's apply this test to the case of Pastor Dan, the busy pastor who's neglecting his sons. What does he feel? Guilt over spending so little time with his boys, seeing to their emotional and spiritual well-being.

Is that feeling reasonable or biblical? Since Proverbs 22, Deuteronomy 6, and other passages call upon parents to train their children in the things of God, a strong case could be made that Dan's guilty feeling is biblical.

Finally, what was Dan's intent? Here we enter deep waters, and only Dan could answer with certainty. If he was truly conflicted over the demands on his time and thought there was simply no way to "be there" more for his sons, perhaps he would be innocent in this area. (He would still need to reexamine his priorities and commitments and somehow *make* time to be a father.) But if he deliberately chose, for whatever reason, to devote more time and energy to his work, to the detriment of his family, his guilty feelings would be valid in this area as well.

As you can see, such an analysis of our guilty feelings, though it may sometimes be painful, can nonetheless help us take a big step forward in being guided by truth rather than emotion. But it's only one step, perhaps a first step, because regardless of what we conclude about ourselves, we still have to deal with the opinions of others. And others, including (especially) other Christians, often add to our sense of feeling guilty and deserving of judgment.

Why that is so is the subject of the next chapter.

# Why Others Often Don't Help

Ungraced people, having little grace to give, become ungracious toward others.... They feel as resentful and angry against the failures of others as they do against their own shortcomings.

DAVID SEAMANDS[1]

The church in which I grew up was a good church in many ways. I learned much about the Bible, grew to love the great hymns of the faith, and met a lot of fine Christian people. I became a Christian myself as a child in its Sunday school.

I also became a legalist there.

It was a church with a lot of rules, mostly about what we couldn't do—especially if, like me, you were part of the family of a church officer. For instance, we couldn't drink, dance, go to movies, or play any kind of card game using a poker deck. Though I heard that God loved me and forgave my sins, I formed the impression over the years that my standing with God—my acceptance with Him, and His availability to me—depended on how well I did at keeping those rules.

Growing out of my legalism, I also became a judgmental person. Nobody said it in so many words, but I developed a strong conviction that we were 100 percent right in our doctrinal beliefs, and everyone else was wrong. Consequently, I believed that lots of people in other churches were bound for hell, and maybe even demon-possessed. Without bothering to try to know them or understand them or their faith, I condemned and then dismissed them in my mind, thankful that I was not as "ignorant" or "misled" as they.

The other churches I attended through my formative years reinforced these views. Not until I had been out of college for several years and found myself working alongside some of those "different" Christians did I start to realize that many of them knew God at least as well as I did, if not better.

Gradually, my understanding grew of God and His grace, and of who He has accepted and forgiven, for which I'm truly grateful.

Many people in our churches today, however, are still where I was—legalistic and judgmental. Usually, they're the ones who don't help us in our desire to feel forgiven—who, in their teaching and casual comments, tend to keep us wallowing in guilt rather than reveling in God's grace. In trying to understand them and why they seem to champion guilty feelings, we can find some answers in a well-known biblical story. In it, Jesus told of someone desperate for grace and of a brother determined instead to condemn.

### A Story of Condemnation, a Story of Grace

A young man had strayed far from his father, both physically and in terms of lifestyle and values. Preferring the company of those who loved only his money to that of his tenderhearted dad, he squandered his inheritance on riotous living. When his cash was gone, along with his "friends," he found himself in despair and finally came to his senses.

Resolved to seek a servant's place on his father's staff, the young man found instead a gracious welcome and the restoration of his rights as a son. Indeed, his dad was so happy to see him that he immediately threw a party to end all parties in celebration of his son's return. The whole household was excited at the safe return of this prodigal son ... all, that is, except for one person.

The young man had an older brother who had been away from the house, working hard, when Junior returned. By the time this brother got home, the party was blazing away. As he approached the house he heard the music and dancing, so he called one of the servants for an explanation.

Understand, this older (and only) brother was going to be crucial to the younger man's peace of mind and sense of acceptance in the family in the days and weeks ahead. After all, he was "big brother," the one who, when they were little, had probably taught Junior how to play games and read a comic book under the covers at night while pretending to be asleep. Now they would be seeing each other and working together every day again. If the older brother shared his father's joy in the younger man's return and made him feel welcome, it would go a long way toward making Junior feel truly forgiven, a fully restored member of the family.

Well, the servant told this older brother what had happened and why this party that could probably be heard to the far side of the county was now under way. And how did the brother respond? Did he, like the shepherd in Jesus' parable who rejoiced over finding his one lost sheep (see Lk 15:3-7), happily call his friends and neighbors together so they could share in his good news?

Not exactly. Actually, not even close to that. Here's how Luke tells the story:

"The older brother became angry and refused to go in. So his father went out and pleaded with him. But he answered his father, 'Look! All these years I've been slaving for you and never disobeyed your orders. Yet you never gave me even a young goat so I could celebrate with my friends. But when this son of yours who has squandered your property with prostitutes comes home, you kill the fattened calf for him!'" (Lk 15:28-30).

In reacting that way, this brother was like so many in the family of God today—our brothers and sisters in Christ—who want to make it hard for us to feel forgiven even when we have sincerely repented of our sins and sought to make amends. His words and his actions capture the attitudes that are all too common in the church. To understand these people better (often it's us!) and why they can make life so difficult, let's look more closely at what was going on with the older brother.

### Unloving Toward His Brother

When the father saw that his younger son had returned safely from his rebellious revelry in a distant country, this dad responded with great joy and a desire to celebrate. Why? Because in spite of all the young man had done, his father still loved him dearly.

When the older brother heard that Junior had returned safely, no joy welled up in his heart. His brother's safe return, and the party that followed, made him angry. Why? Clearly, he did not share his father's love for his brother.

Chances are, they hadn't gotten along very well even before the younger man took his share of the estate and left the family farm. Little brother's decision, and the motivation behind it, only strained the relationship further. When their father agreed to Junior's request, the older brother likely thought it was both unwise and indulgent. (Unlike their father, he didn't understand that love cannot be compelled.) Later, reports about how Junior was squandering his money and disgracing the family must have added to the older brother's growing, burning hatred toward his sibling.

In a similar way, judgmental people today tend to be unloving toward those they judge. They don't "rejoice with those who rejoice" or "mourn with those who mourn" (Rom 12:15). They're strangers to compassion, aliens to mercy. They read a verse like John 13:34—"A new command I give you: Love one another. As I have loved you, so you must love one another"—and, practically speaking, they haven't got a clue about what that means. They're motivated more by a desire to compel conformity to their rules than by any sense of real compassion.

### Unloving Toward the Father

Not only was the older brother unloving toward his younger sibling, but he was also unloving toward his father. Oh, if you had asked him directly, he probably would have said something like, "What do you mean? Of course I love my father! After all, I'm the one who stayed with him and followed in his footsteps!"

But notice what he told his dad in the heat of the moment:

"Look! All these years I've been *slaving* for you" (emphasis added)—not "working with you" or "sharing life with you." That statement betrayed his true feelings. He may have stayed at his father's side over the years, but his heart was far from him. Being close physically did not translate into fellowship and love. Instead, he saw his time with his father as servitude, himself as a slave rather than a son.

Today, those who want us to continue feeling guilty are just the same. They don't love God so much as they fear Him; they fear Him as much as they say the rest of us should. They see themselves as indentured servants, trying to pay for their sins, in effect denying the sufficiency of Jesus' payment on their behalf. They have a great sense of duty toward their heavenly Father, but little sense of affection.

## A Superiority Complex

Besides hating Junior, the older brother obviously thought himself superior to him. In spirit if not in actuality, he was a Pharisee, just like those who confronted Jesus. "All these years," he told their father, "I've ... never disobeyed your orders." And the implication followed, "... unlike that other, rebellious, thoroughly disgraced sinner-son of yours."

No doubt many of his future conversations with his sibling were going to begin with the words, "*I* never would have..." And again the implication would be, "because I'm too good, too righteous, too obedient for that." Or put another way, "I'm better than you; I'm more righteous than you; I'm more faithful than you."

Still today, modern Pharisees are in the business of comparison and of finding themselves superior to those who admit their faults. Indeed, concluding that they're better than others is one way they make themselves feel more comfortable with their own shortcomings. When they say, "There but for the grace of God go I," they are expressing not compassion but condescension. And their attitude comes through loud and clear.

Lewis Smedes says of such Christians, "Self-righteous people do not want you to forgive yourself. They want you to walk forever under the black umbrella of permanent shame."[2] But as we'll discuss later, we don't have to comply with their desire. We can choose instead to walk in the sunshine of God's grace.

### Resentful

Next, after declaring his superiority over Junior, the older brother showed he resented the way his brother's return was being celebrated. "You never gave me even a young goat so I could celebrate with my friends," he told their father.

Now, had Dad really never given this firstborn son a party in his honor or a chance to celebrate with his friends? That's highly doubtful; the father played no favorites with his sons whom he loved equally. So this older brother was almost certainly exaggerating. His was a statement not of fact but of the resentment he felt toward his sibling. As far as he was concerned, Junior's return was no cause for festivity.

In all likelihood, this older brother simply didn't believe Junior's "conversion" was genuine. He probably figured

Junior was just resting up and waiting for the chance to ask Dad for more money so he could go off on another binge of sinful living.

Likewise in the present time, many believers are skeptical when they hear of the conversion of a sinner (especially a prominent one) or of the repentance of a fallen Christian leader. No doubt some professions of faith and statements of confession are *not* entirely genuine. Yet the skepticism of these people is almost an automatic, unthinking reaction. It's as if they assume God *can't* get through to certain people whose offenses are so bad as to make them—in the eyes of these judges—irredeemable. And that can include most anyone.

When we encounter these skeptical Christians, resentful of God's grace extended to the "unworthy," they can suck the air right out of any celebration of God's grace.

I remember when a prominent Christian leader publicly confessed to having committed sexual sin. He announced at the time that he would step down from his position and submit himself to a process of discipline, accountability, and—he hoped—eventual restoration supervised by godly people.

Although saddened by the revelation, since this was someone I had admired greatly, I thought he sounded truly repentant, and that his proposed course of action was biblical. All around me, however, I heard Christians saying things like, "He's just the same as all the rest! He has no business ever preaching or being in leadership again!"

Frankly, their lack of grace and their unwillingness to consider even the possibility that God might have some further public ministry for the man in the future saddened me even more.

## Unforgiving and Judgmental

As the older brother's next words reveal, being skeptical and resentful was only the beginning of his negative attitude toward his sibling. "But when this son of yours who has squandered your property with prostitutes comes home," he said, "you kill the fattened calf for him!"

Clearly, he had not forgiven Junior for his many sins. Instead, in his own mind and heart, he had long ago tried his younger brother, judged him guilty, and sentenced him to eternal banishment from the family. Now he was ready to carry out the sentence. If it had been up to him, rather than having the servants prepare a feast of celebration, he would have had them drive Junior off the property with stones and spears.

This unloving, self-righteous, unforgiving older brother wasn't about to let Junior off the hook, at least not so easily. Indeed, the servant who had told the older brother the reason for the party hadn't even mentioned Junior's repentant attitude; he had merely said the father was rejoicing over the safe return of his son.

*How can this be?* the older brother must have reasoned. *Has Dad developed a sudden case of amnesia? How could he have forgotten what Junior did? This is our chance to punish him for what he did, not throw a party!*

Our unforgiving brothers and sisters today will likewise want to judge rather than forgive, to punish rather than extend grace. They themselves have labored mightily to be faithful to God; how can He then pardon those who have put forth little or no such effort? They seem to think, therefore, that it's their assignment from God to mete out His justice. And, of course, they're always sure of the rightness and the righteousness of their judgments.

As far as these folks are concerned, no statement or sign of repentance is sufficient. They won't be satisfied until a sinner has received what he "deserves," if even then. They insist that the sinner "pay the price" for his or her offenses, somehow forgetting that this is precisely what Jesus came to do on that sinner's behalf.

### Ignorant of His Relationship With the Father

In responding to the older brother's complaint, the father kindly pointed out that this child of his didn't really understand their relationship. "My son," he said, "you are always with me, and everything I have is yours" (Lk 15:31). Did this son, a grown man, really need to hear such a simple, basic truth? Yes, he did, because despite being with his father all his life, he apparently had never realized what was his.

If this older son had ever wanted a celebration of his own—a sign of his father's love and devotion—it was his for the asking. In fact, his dad would have been delighted to give it. Unlike the younger son, who was out of touch and out of the father's reach for so long, this older son could have enjoyed the father's embrace at any time. Only his own ignorance kept him from it—that and his hardness of heart.

### Out of Fellowship With the Father

In his final words, his last effort to make his judgmental, hard-hearted son (whom he nonetheless loved) understand, this father of *two* rebellious children poured out his own heart. "But we *had* to celebrate and be glad," he exclaimed, "because this brother of yours was dead and is alive again; he was lost and is found" (Lk 15:32, emphasis added).

Here was the father's love laid bare. As far as he was concerned—and certainly from a spiritual standpoint—his younger son had been dead, and now he was alive again! He had been lost—a priceless treasure—and now was found again! How could the father and those who shared his heart and his values not make merry?

They couldn't, and that's why the older son wanted no part in their celebration.

All those years he had spent with his father, even while his younger sibling was in the far country of rebellion, and yet his heart was no closer to the father than his brother's. Indeed, when the repentant younger man came home to his dad's loving embrace, he was much more like his father than the older son (who had only gone through the superficial motions of sonship) had ever been. The fellowship they could now enjoy was boundless, while the older brother could only look on longingly, resentfully, from outside the wall he had built between himself and the father.

What a tragedy! To be in the presence of the unconditional love that every human being craves and yet unable to accept it for yourself! And because of that, unable to extend it to others.

This, too, is the plight of our judgmental brothers and sisters in Christ. They've never understood and never accepted God's unconditional love for themselves, so they can't offer it to others. Sinners are candidates for wrath and perhaps penitence, they believe, but not for grace; when sinners try to "come home," the judgmental condemn.

## An Attitude Often Learned Early

Since the father in Jesus' parable was so loving and forgiving, how did the prodigal's older brother get to be such an unloving legalist? He didn't learn it at home, but there were no doubt plenty of judgmental role models around for him to choose from. And his father may well have had friends like Job's comforters dropping in every day, advising him to come down like a load of bricks on his younger son if he ever returned. "Spare the rod, spoil the child," they would have chanted.

Unfortunately, judgmentalism—toward others *and* ourselves—is an attitude that's often learned early in life. Unlike the prodigal's brother, most of us get it from our parents, because it's the way they were raised by their parents, who were raised that way by *their* parents, and so on. As Christian psychiatrist Dr. Paul Tournier pointed out after years of professional practice and observation, "All upbringing is a cultivation of the sense of guilt on an intensive scale. Especially the best education, that by parents who are most anxious about the moral training of children and their success in life."[3]

In other words, our loving parents, who want to teach us to "be good" even when they're not around, do so by developing in us a strong sense of guilt over anything we do "bad"— as they've defined it. And their definition of *bad* is usually very broad, going so far beyond a biblical sense of right and wrong as to include things like how we arrange the table for dinner. This sets us up to judge ourselves and others quickly and harshly when we or they violate our childhood training.

It also sets us up to experience a lot of false guilt.

Then there are those parents who believe—and who teach

their children—that anything enjoyable is sinful. Dr. Tournier wrote of them, "Many people have told me how this idea from their upbringing has lingered on. It was inculcated like an inexorable adage: 'Enjoyment prohibited.' They can enjoy nothing without feeling conscience-stricken and this spoils their pleasure."[4]

Those of us who had such parents are almost guaranteed to feel guilty most of the time, often because we "dared" to enjoy purely innocent pleasures. This, too, is false guilt, but it's tough to deal with not only because it was deeply ingrained in childhood, but also because resolving it means facing the painful conclusion that the mom and dad we love and respect were wrong about one of life's key truths.

## In the Church

In the story of the prodigal's older brother, we saw the same attitudes of many in the church who want to keep us feeling guilty: unloving, condescending, resentful, unforgiving, legalistic, and judgmental. But that's not the whole story. Many well-intentioned but misguided Christians, for example, truly believe that legalism (acceptance based on performance) is the only way to keep people in line, to keep them from sinning continually. As my own pastor puts it, "You'll hear people say that if you emphasize grace too much, people will go wild."

The legalists reason like this: "The doctrine of grace says that God's acceptance of us is not based on our merit—on how well we do or don't behave according to His standard—but solely on His love for us and the price Jesus paid on the cross to redeem us. No matter what we do, we are accepted in the Beloved. But if we talk about that too much, people will take advantage of it. They'll feel free to sin, knowing that God forgives them regardless. We've got to rein them in!"

And it's true that some Christians will argue, "If our sin gives God the opportunity to display more of His grace, let's just go on sinning." The apostle Paul confronted this mind-set in the early days of the church. "Where sin increased, grace increased all the more," he acknowledged in Romans 5:20. Then he addressed the question head-on: "What shall we say, then? Shall we go on sinning so that grace may increase?" (Rom 6:1).

But notice his answer. Did he say that continued sinning would bring down God's wrath on us? No. Did he say that it's the job of church leaders to emphasize Christian duty more than grace in order to keep people under control? No. Rather, he appealed to our understanding of our relationship with God.

In the rest of Romans 6 and the early part of chapter 7, Paul used three word pictures to portray how we are now connected to God: baptism, slavery, and marriage.

Regarding baptism he said, "Don't you know that all of us who were baptized into Christ Jesus were baptized into his death? We were therefore buried with him through baptism into death in order that, just as Christ was raised from the dead through the glory of the Father, we too may live a new life" (6:3-4). Therefore, since we have this new life in Christ, "count yourselves dead to sin but alive to God in Christ Jesus" (v. 11).

When we were baptized into Christ Jesus by the Holy Spirit (see 1 Cor 12:13), we died to the power of sin and came alive to God. It's a done deal, a finished fact. We just need to remember it and act as if it's true.

Regarding slavery he said, "Don't you know that when you

offer yourselves to someone to obey him as slaves, you are slaves to the one whom you obey—whether you are slaves to sin, which leads to death, or to obedience, which leads to righteousness? But thanks be to God that, though you used to be slaves to sin, you wholeheartedly obeyed the form of teaching to which you were entrusted. You have been set free from sin and have become slaves to righteousness" (Rom 6:16-18).

The bad news, to our independent way of thinking, is that there's no such thing as total autonomy. All people are slaves—either to sin or to God's righteousness. The good news is that those of us who have believed in Christ now have a Master who is determined to bless us rather than destroy us (the goal of our old master).

Regarding marriage he said, "For example, by law a married woman is bound to her husband as long as he is alive, but if her husband dies, she is released from the law of marriage.... So, my brothers, you also died to the law through the body of Christ, that you might belong to another, to him who was raised from the dead, in order that we might bear fruit to God" (Rom 7:2, 4).

Before, we were "married" to the law, which condemned us because of our inability to obey it perfectly. (Imagine trying to live with a spouse who continually reminds you of how bad you are!) Now we're wed to Christ (who died to secure our forgiveness once and for all time), and our love and loyalty are rightfully His.

In all three cases, the point is that our faith in Christ has fundamentally and forever changed our relationship with both sin and our Savior. We have died to sin and are now alive to Him; we are His bride and, yes, His slaves (also His brothers and sisters, not to mention fellow priests, among other images used by the New Testament writers). *That's* why we try now to live as He would in our place.

## No Escape

It isn't just the legalists in the church who can make us feel guilty, either. Even kind-intentioned people who merely want to share their own success stories can add to our burden. Hoping to help a fellow believer who is struggling in some way, they'll say, "If you'll only do things this way ... If you'll only pray that way (or with that attitude) ... If you'll only trust God more ... If you'll only have more faith ..."

The typical effect of these testimonies and exhortations, especially if we already feel guilty, is to make us feel even *more* guilty. Why? Because we're being told now that in addition to whatever else we're struggling with, we also don't know how to act, pray, trust, or have faith like a "good" Christian. We've been misinformed or, worse still, we're inadequate—guilt piled upon guilt.

The good intentions have backfired.

Everywhere we turn, someone, for some reason or other, is trying to make us feel guilty. The majority of our fellow Christians, it seems, do not have a practical grasp on God's grace for themselves, so they're not willing or able to let others enjoy it. Understanding that such people are all around us in our churches, we can prepare ourselves to resist their pressure to conform and feel guilty. But it's not as if they're the only reason we struggle to feel forgiven. Another is that we, ourselves, find it hard to believe that anyone, including God, could really love us unconditionally.

We will look next at why that is so.

# Our Struggle to Accept Unconditional Love

What comes into our minds when we think about God is the most important thing about us.

A.W. TOZER[1]

If there's one place in the world where we'd like to think we can always find unconditional love, it's from our parents—especially dear old Mom. Of course, that's not always the case.

Consider a woman named Bethany and her family who struggled day in and day out with an aggressive, misbehaving child. No matter what form of discipline they tried, six-year-old Steven could not be controlled. This was true in school and in public, as well as in the privacy of the family's home. Consequently, Bethany said, "I've cried many days on my job, at home, and on my knees in prayer … feeling … like I was a bad mother."

Now, it's no surprise that neighbors, school officials, and other parents would make this woman feel guilty over her son's misconduct (which, by the way, was eventually diagnosed as being the result of attention deficit disorder). But surely her own mother would be understanding and supportive, right?

Wrong. Bethany went on to say, *"I've been ridiculed by my mother as a bad parent* and pitied so much by others that many times I've wanted to pack up and move to where nobody knows us."

Then there was a man named George who sinned but thought that if he confessed and repented, he could find grace—undergirded by love—in his local church. He had engaged in an adulterous affair, a serious offense to be sure. But when he came to his senses, like the Prodigal Son in Jesus' parable, he confessed it to his wife and asked for her forgiveness. She, not unreasonably, insisted that he go to their pastor for counseling.

In the pastor's office, George again confessed his sin and then said, "I want to begin living with integrity before God, my wife, and the church. I really want to mature as a Christian, and I'm willing to be held accountable for my future actions. Would you help me?"

Unfortunately, the pastor's response was devoid of grace or any hint of love, full instead of harshness and legalism. George later reported, "The only counseling I got was a wave of his finger in my face, and restoration through works."

In these two brief stories, we have prime examples of one of the chief reasons we struggle mightily to accept God's unconditional love extended through Jesus Christ. Namely, we rarely if ever encounter such love in our human experience, and that makes it hard to believe His love is really different. As a result, we continue to be mired in the feeling that we are condemned rather than loved; that we still bear the guilt of our sins, both real and imagined.

## Fleeting Human Love

Far from being unconditional, most human love is fleeting. It can evaporate seemingly in an instant, as soon as we do or say something of which the other person disapproves. And society as a whole grants or withholds its approval based on how we measure up to standards that are constantly changing and often impossible for most of us to attain.

Henri Nouwen, the priest, professor, and prolific author, explains the situation this way: "In a world that constantly compares people, ranking them as more or less intelligent, more or less attractive, more or less successful, it is not easy to really believe in a love [God's] that does not do the same."[2]

The world isn't subtle, either, in its attempt to convince us we aren't worthy of being loved. Nouwen, seeing himself as the Prodigal Son of Luke 15, continues:

The dark voices of my surrounding world try to persuade me that I am no good and that I can only become good by earning my goodness through "making it" up the ladder of success. These voices lead me quickly to forget the voice that calls me "my son, the Beloved," reminding me of my being loved independently of any acclaim or accomplishment. These dark voices drown out that gentle, soft, light-giving voice ...; they drag me to the periphery of my existence and make me doubt that there is a loving God waiting for me at the very center of my being.[3]

Obviously, of course, some people are much more capable of giving love than others. But the fact is that no one except God can love totally unconditionally—perfectly—because only He is perfect. The rest of us get angry, hurt, disappointed, proud, or just plain selfish. And thus we find it hard to imagine that the same isn't true of God as well. We simply can't fathom "a heart that does not demand anything for itself, a heart that is completely empty of self-seeking."[4]

## Our Longing for God's Love

The great irony in this is that we desperately, instinctively need and want God's love. We understand, as the catechism says, that we were made to know Him and enjoy Him forever. If we have put our faith in His gospel of grace, we've tasted at least a little of His love, and our souls yearn for more.

Indeed, as our pangs of guilt remind us frequently, if God is unable or unwilling to love us unconditionally, then we are truly and surely without hope. That's why any and all religions that challenge us to be good enough or do enough good works to satisfy a holy God must ultimately end in despair. We are utterly incapable of saving ourselves; we will never be good enough, even if we should somehow live a thousand years. Our *only* hope is in the mercy and love shown by a God willing to sacrifice His own Son to pay the penalty for our sins.

It isn't just Christians, either, who feel the need of God's love. As Solomon put it, God "has also set eternity in the hearts of men" (Eccl 3:11). We all know intuitively, as Paul said to the unbelieving Athenians, that "in him we live and move and have our being" (Acts 17:28).

Because we have that basic, innate understanding of our need to be rightly related to our Creator (though many today try to deny it), we also are anxious about being out of His favor. Psychiatrist Paul Tournier explained, "Fear of losing the love of God—this is the essence of our human problem and of psychology. Even a person who does not believe in God, trembles to lose His love."[5]

The periodic, wide-scale rediscovery of just how great His love is, on the other hand, lights the fires of what we commonly call "revival." In the words of Dr. Tournier, "Suddenly there dawns upon us the vast, entire endowment of God's free love and forgiveness, and of the reconciliation He offers us in Jesus Christ. It is this which bowls us over, frees us from the burden of guilt, transforms us.... It is this discovery which periodically in history gives rise to an outburst of infectious faith, mass conversions and irrepressible joy."[6]

Yet, even having accepted God's gracious gift of salvation, we struggle to accept His love. We've looked already at one reason this is so. Another is that we routinely misconstrue this Lord who has labored mightily to make plain the nature of His love.

### Misunderstanding God

There's no mystery about the most common misunderstanding of God, even among those who are saved. Pastor Glenn Wagner speaks almost universally when he says, "I meet Christians all the time who view God as the Deity sitting up in heaven holding a baseball bat, ready to club them for every false move they make."[7]

Nor is this lie of the devil only a modern misconception. Herman Melville hit the same nail on the head more than a hundred years ago when he wrote, "The reason the mass of men dislike God and at the bottom fear Him is because they fancy Him all brain, like a watch."[8] In other words, He's just a heartless judge, ruling the world without compassion.

Betsy Nagelsen McCormack, a former professional tennis player, gave a good illustration of this mind-set in a recent appearance on *The 700 Club*. She became a Christian at the age of sixteen, she said, yet for many years thereafter she lived with the expectation that she had to be spiritually perfect. If she couldn't meet that standard (which, of course, she couldn't), she believed she couldn't really be a child of God. That is, she couldn't truly be loved and accepted by Him.

Thus, even though she had placed her faith in Jesus Christ and asked Him to be her Savior from sin, she still felt insecure in His love. She couldn't escape the nagging fear that He was judging her rather than offering to embrace her. Only in recent years had she begun to better appreciate His grace.

Unfortunately, this misconception about God is widespread. A majority of Christians seem to labor under it, and virtually all of us are tempted to believe it at least occasionally. And if we're thinking of Him as angry and judgmental, waiting to jump on us every time we slip, of course we're going to struggle to believe He loves us unconditionally.

Henri Nouwen captured the feelings generated by this struggle when he wrote, again in the context of the Prodigal Son story, "I still think about his [God's] love as conditional and about home [His presence] as a place I am not yet fully sure of. While walking home, I keep entertaining doubts about whether I will be truly welcome when I get there. As I look at my spiritual journey, my long and fatiguing trip home, I see how full it is of guilt about the past and worries about the future.... Belief in total, absolute forgiveness does not come readily."[9]

Indeed it does not, when at the level of our feelings we view God as a lumbering ogre rather than as the lover of our souls.

## The Issue of Control

Still another reason we have trouble accepting God's unconditional love and so continue to wallow in guilt is that we understand, implicitly if not explicitly, that drawing near to Him means surrendering control of our lives. And we don't give up that control easily, even when we know intellectually that He has only our best interests at heart. Therefore, a part of us tends to want to keep a certain "safe" distance from Him.

Scripture makes it plain that when we place ourselves in God's hands and cooperate with His will for our lives, He will set about molding us into the image of His Son in various ways, including many that we will find unpleasant at the time. He loves us too much to leave us as we are. Hebrews 12:5-12, for example, tells us,

And you have forgotten that word of encouragement that addresses you as sons: "My son, do not make light of the Lord's discipline, and do not lose heart when he rebukes you, because the Lord disciplines those he loves, and he punishes everyone he accepts as a son." Endure hardship as discipline; God is treating you as sons. For what son is not disciplined by his father? If you are not disciplined (and everyone undergoes discipline), then you are illegitimate children and not true sons. Moreover, we have all had human fathers who disciplined us and we respected them for it. How much more should we submit to the Father of our spirits and live! Our fathers disciplined us for a little while as they thought best; but God disciplines us for our good, that we may share in his holiness. No discipline seems pleasant at the time, but painful. Later on, however, it produces a harvest of righteousness and peace for those who have been trained by it. Therefore, strengthen your feeble arms and weak knees.

God is about the business of preparing us for an eternity of fellowship with Himself, a glorious goal and a high calling. But the process is often painful, and a part of us shrinks from it. C.S. Lewis captured this reality in a couple of word pictures that have stayed with me for years, ever since I first read them.

First, he said that we usually go to God like a person with a toothache going to the dentist: We're just looking for immediate relief from the pain. The dentist, however, has the "big picture" in view and will start with the sore tooth but then move on to examine the entire mouth, very likely finding other problems that need attention as well. Knowing that and not wanting to "take our medicine," we put off going to the dentist as long as we can, even in the face of considerable pain.

God is like the dentist. We may ask for His help with a particular sin problem of which we're ashamed. Lewis continued,

Well, He will cure it all right, but He will not stop there. That may be all you asked; but if once you call Him in, He will give you the full treatment. That is why He warned people to "count the cost" before becoming Christians. "Make no mistake," He says, "if you let Me, I will make you perfect. The moment you put yourself in My hands, that is what you are in for. Nothing less, or other, than that.

You have free will, and if you choose, you can push Me away. But if you do not push Me away, understand that I am going to see this job through.... This I can do and will do. But I will not do anything less.[10]

Lewis' second word picture, which he borrowed from George MacDonald, is even more vivid:

Imagine yourself as a living house. God comes in to rebuild that house. At first, perhaps, you can understand what He is doing. He is getting the drains right and stopping the leaks in the roof and so on: you knew that those jobs needed doing and so you are not surprised. But presently He starts knocking the house about in a way that hurts abominably and does not seem to make sense. What on earth is He up to? The explanation is that He is building quite a different house from the one you thought of—throwing out a new wing here, putting on an extra floor there, running up towers, making courtyards. You thought you were going to be made into a decent little cottage: but He is building a palace. He intends to come and live in it Himself.[11]

In short, God has given us the privilege of being His children by grace (see, for example, Gal 4:4-7), and because He loves us, He is not content to leave us as we are. Instead, He is intent on making us more and more like His Son: "For those God foreknew he also predestined to be conformed to the likeness of his Son, that he might be the firstborn among many brothers" (Rom 8:29). This is an ongoing and sometimes painful process, as Hebrews 12 and other scriptures reveal. Knowing that, we hesitate to run into His loving embrace.

## Learning to Let God Love Us

If letting God love us is such a challenge, how do we do it? How do we overcome the lack of good human models, clarify our understanding of God, and reach a point of being willing to surrender control? How do we replace our fear of God with a deep-in-the-gut conviction that He truly loves us and has forgiven our failures? How do we come to the point, like the Prodigal Son, that we believe that being in His presence is better than being in the far country—enough so that we put our belief into action?

My prayer is that this entire book will serve to nurture our appreciation for the unfathomable depth of God's love and grace. But it may also help right now to contemplate for a few moments the incredible price He paid to secure our forgiveness, and what that says about how much He must love us.

Think with me about this: The eternal, holy, Creator God made us out of the dust of the earth and put us (the human race, in the form of our ancestors Adam and Eve) in a perfect setting, the Garden of Eden. There He fellowshiped with us, Friend to friend, every day. But we rebelled. We turned our backs on His love, spurning His presence. We believed the lies of the serpent rather than the truth of our Maker. We chose spiritual death over life with Him.

How did He respond? With a heavy sigh and a "That's too bad, but they made their choice, and now they have to live with it"? With anger and a "Good riddance to bad rubbish"? With a self-pitying "How could they do this to Me"?

No, the Bible tells us that our Father God prepared to send His only begotten Son into the world He had created so that the Son could pay the penalty for our sin and make possible our forgiveness and reconciliation with Him. The Son would do that by letting us nail Him to a tree and shed His blood.

In fact, the Bible tells us that even before He made the world and everything in it, God knew we would rebel and was already determined to make that sacrifice on our behalf. *Before we ever existed, He loved us enough to die for us.* Revelation 13:8 describes the Son as "the Lamb that was slain from the creation of the world." Or as I once heard it put, the moment Adam and Eve first bit into the forbidden fruit, Jesus prepared to leave for Bethlehem.

If you're a parent yourself, let me ask you: Would you be willing to let your child die for a traitor? How about for a thief? for a gangster? for an adulterer? for a rapist? for a mass murderer? As a father, my own immediate response to all those is "No way." Maybe, on a good day spiritually, I would be willing to lay down my own life to save one of them. But offer my son to die so they wouldn't have to? Frankly, I don't think so.

The Bible explains, however, that God answered the same question, "Yes, absolutely!"

Here's some of what it says:

You see, at just the right time, when we were still powerless, Christ died for the ungodly. Very rarely will anyone die for a righteous man, though for a good man someone might possibly dare to die. *But God demonstrates his own love for us in this: While we were still sinners, Christ died for us.* Since we have now been justified by his blood, how much more shall we be saved from God's wrath through him! For if, when we were God's enemies, we were reconciled to him through the death of his Son, how much more, having been reconciled, shall we be saved through his life! Not only is this so, but we also rejoice in God through our Lord Jesus Christ, through whom we have now received reconciliation.

ROMANS 5:6-11, emphasis added

While we were still in rebellion against Him, God the Father sent His only Son, and God the Son willingly humbled Himself to come, to pay our penalty by dying the death we deserved.

Pastor and author Max Lucado tells a story about one time going to collect his two oldest daughters after they had been away at summer camp for a week. Even though they had been gone only seven days, he had missed them so much that he flew up a day early just to make sure he wouldn't be late. When the time came the next day for the parents to enter the camp and get their children, he says, "I was ready for this moment. I had waited long enough.... Good thing I was wearing jogging shoes. I broke into a run. Enough preliminaries. The hour had struck and the rope was down, and I was willing to do what it took to see my kids."

Then he continues, "God feels the same. God is ready to see his own.... He, too, will do whatever is necessary to take them home. Yet, his desire leaves ours in the dust.... I went from the state of Texas to the state of Missouri. He went from the state of being worshiped in heaven to being a baby in Bethlehem."[12]

Whatever was necessary to reconcile us to Himself, the God of this entire universe was willing to do. And what was necessary was the sacrifice of His only Son. That's unmerited favor—in a word, *grace*. That's unconditional love—we didn't earn it before and can't now. That's the love God has for us.

Imagine Jesus, as He was about to be bolted to the cross, looking tenderly at you and saying, "I want to do this for you." Then imagine Him on Easter morning, extending nail-pierced hands to you and offering, "Come and join me in the Father's gracious presence—for all eternity."

Think about that for a while.

Marvel at such love.

Marvel at such a God.

And marvel at the fact that such a God extends such love to *you*.

Sit quietly and meditate on His incredible love for a few minutes. Ask the Holy Spirit to sink it into the very core of your being. Let it fill your soul and swell your heart with joy. And then bow before Him in thanksgiving.

### Childlike Faith

One day, a boy about eight years old walked up to the front door of a house and rang the doorbell. Another boy the same age answered the bell, and the first boy said, "I'm sorry about what happened. Can we be friends again?"

Now, how do you suppose the second boy responded? If he had been like many adults, he might have said, "I'll have to think about it." Or he could have said, "I'm still hurting too much. Maybe when the wound has had time to heal." He might even have shot back, "No way! Get off my porch and don't ever come back! I never want to see your ugly face again!"

But since he was a child, he instead said without hesitation,

"Okay. Do you have Micro Machines?"

And just like that, they were buddies again.

Is it too much to hope that we grown-ups could someday come to a point of being able to seek and accept God's love and forgiveness as simply and easily?

Jesus said, "I tell you the truth, anyone who will not receive the kingdom of God like a little child will never enter it" (Mk 10:15). Like a little child—in pure, trusting faith, taking God at His word, believing that what He says about His love and acceptance of us is true. Can we believe and trust Him that way?

"When will we ever learn?" Chuck Swindoll wrote. "God *delights* in choosing those most unworthy [that's you and me] and making them the objects of His unconditional acceptance."[13]

The story is told of a Chinese woman who heard the gospel for the first time, the truth of God's limitless love for and complete acceptance of those who put their faith in His Son, Jesus Christ. Her simple but profound response was, "I knew there ought to be a God like that somewhere."[14]

The good news—the fact upon which you can stake your life both now and forever—is that such a God does exist, and He loves *you*.

# The Problem of Habitual Sin

A guilty conscience needs no accuser.

ANONYMOUS

One of our greatest problems with feeling forgiven arises when we find ourselves constantly battling some kind of habitual sin. Each time we fail, we feel fresh guilt for the new offense against God, plus a renewal of our ongoing guilt over our inability to get the habit under control.

*Why can't I stop doing this?* we wonder. *Where is the "Christ living in me" that the Bible talks about?* And we conclude in despair, *God has to be getting pretty fed up with me. I just hope He isn't ready to write me off as hopeless.*

I confess that I have a sinful habit of my own. It flares anew almost every time I'm by myself in my car. Some of my worst moments spiritually, in fact, come when I'm behind the wheel. Ordinarily, I'm an even-tempered person. And if others are in the car with me, my self-control usually remains strong. But when I'm alone in the driver's seat, it's another story altogether.

For some reason, when it's just me and the steering wheel, even minor hassles can spur an angry outburst. A light turning red just as I approach (especially if I'm in a hurry); a driver who cuts into the safety zone I've left between my car and the one in front of me; drivers who ride my tail, wanting me to go faster when I'm already doing the speed limit (where *are* the cops when you need them?)—any of these can start me growling inside the privacy of my car, often with profanity.

I'm reminded of what Solomon wrote in the book of Proverbs: "A fool gives full vent to his anger, but a wise man keeps himself under control" (29:11). So when I lose my temper in the car, I guess that makes me ...

"Like a city whose walls are broken down [i.e., defenseless against enemies; in big trouble] is a man who lacks self-control," Solomon added in Proverbs 25:28.

"No man can tame the tongue," the apostle James said. "It is a restless evil, full of deadly poison" (James 3:8). And that certainly has been my experience, at least when by myself in an automobile.

Then James went on to say, "With the tongue we praise our Lord and Father, and with it we curse men, who have been made in God's likeness. Out of the same mouth come praise and cursing. My brothers, this should not be" (Jas 3:9-10).

All I want to know is, did James somehow look into the future and see me driving before he wrote that? But of course, the answer is that my difficulty controlling my tongue is common to all people in all ages, and the beauty of the Bible is that it speaks to each of us individually at our point of need. I clearly need help in this area, because reading such verses makes me feel guilty all over again, even though I confess and repent of the sin every time.

As I said at the beginning of this chapter, my (our) guilty feelings related to a sinful habit are of two kinds. First, I feel fresh guilt every time I lose control of my temper and utter a profanity. Second, the underlying, chronic guilt I feel over still not having the habit whipped after all these years flares anew.

Perhaps you can relate to my temper and foul mouth. Or perhaps you struggle with some other kind of habitual sin, some area of your life in which you constantly fail. It's not a matter of violating someone else's preference or opinion—you can point right to the passage of Scripture that you're in the habit of disobeying.

Well, I've got bad news and good news about this common situation.

First, the bad news: Whatever our areas of frequent defeat, the plain fact is that until we begin to make substantial progress in them, we're going to feel guilty *as we should,* because we are guilty of those fresh offenses against God's holiness. We can (and should) always claim the promise of 1 John 1:9 and receive His cleansing, which puts the actual guilt of the sin behind us, but the guilty *feelings* are going to persist as long as the habits last.

Second, the good news: We don't have to go on living in defeat and guilty misery. We can begin to make steady progress in overcoming sinful habits. That can be hard to believe when we're mired in a sinful habit, yet there is hope in God's provision for victory.

## Intended for Victory

The apostle Paul wrote, "We died to sin; how can we live in it any longer?" (Rom 6:2). That isn't mere rhetoric; it's a statement of fundamental fact about our spiritual lives. When we became Christians through faith in Jesus Christ, we died to the power of sin and came alive to the power of God that now resides in us through the person of the indwelling Holy Spirit. Paul put it this way in Galatians 2:20: "I have been crucified with Christ and I no longer live, but Christ lives in me. The life I live in the body, I live by faith in the Son of God, who loved me and gave himself for me."

That means that whereas before we were slaves to sin (see Rom 6:6) and had no choice but to obey it, we can now decide instead to follow the Spirit's leading and live in a way that pleases God. But we have to believe that and act accordingly. That's why Paul went on to say in Romans 6:11 that we should think of ourselves as dead to sin—entirely removed from its power over us—but alive to God. In other words, we need to remember the facts, even when we've failed in the same area for the tenth time in a week (or a day). Remember who and Whose we are. And act consistently with that truth.

Thus, when Paul issued the command in the next two verses not to offer our bodies to sin but to offer ourselves instead to God, he wasn't demanding the impossible. And he provided this familiar supporting promise in 1 Corinthians 10:13: "No temptation has seized you except what is common to man. And God is faithful; he will not let you be tempted beyond what you can bear. But when you are tempted, he will also provide a way out so that you can stand up under it." Notice that he *didn't* say God will keep us from being tempted. But he *did* say God will keep us from being tempted beyond our ability to resist it and do the right thing, and he said God will provide a way out of each temptation.

Now, what will that way out be? What will it look like? There is no easy, simple answer to those questions. The way out will vary from individual to individual and situation to situation, and it may involve more than one element. It's a subject that could fill volumes by itself. But if we believe that God will, indeed, be faithful to provide such a way in every temptation, we will look diligently for it, and our ability to recognize it and use it with the help of the Spirit will grow over time as we are more and more conformed to the image of His Son (see Rom 8:29).

As we go through this process of spiritual growth, which includes the development of self-control in the area of habits, we have other promises from which we can draw strength as well. For example, Paul wrote, "For God did not give us a spirit of timidity, but a spirit of power, of love and of *self-discipline*" (2 Tm 1:7, emphasis added). The capacity for self-discipline, and the power, are already in us as the redeemed children of God.

Paul also wrote, "Being confident of this, that he who began a good work in you *will carry it on to completion* until the day of Christ Jesus" (Phil 1:6, emphasis added). God is absolutely committed to our spiritual growth, to our maturing to be more and more like Jesus. No matter how many times we stumble along the way, we can be confident that the sovereign God *will* carry that work on throughout this lifetime and eventually to completion in heaven.

## Our Part and God's

As we look at the issue of overcoming sinful habits, a question naturally arises: What part does God play, and what must we do? We often hear advice about this that seems to conflict. Some people suggest that all the responsibility for changing us rests on God, so we just "let go and let God." Others say that once we've been set free from the power of sin at the moment of conversion, it's up to us to exercise the free will God gave us and make the right choices.

As is usually the case in a debate among Christians, Scripture can be cited to support both sides of the argument. So which view is right? Without getting into a heavy theological discussion, my answer is that both are correct to some extent.

Certainly, there are some things that only God can do. Only He, for instance, can know us and our circumstances thoroughly and provide that way of escape from temptation every time. Only He can direct the events of our daily lives, which is why Jesus taught us to pray, "And lead us not into temptation, but deliver us from the evil one" (Mt 6:13). God is even responsible for arranging opportunities for us to do good: "For we are God's workmanship, created in Christ Jesus to do good works, *which God prepared in advance for us to do*" (Eph 2:10, emphasis added).

Likewise, God is the one who gives us the desire to obey His will. "For it is God who works in you *to will and to act* according to his good purpose," we read in Philippians 2:13 (emphasis added). And it's His power, through the resident Holy Spirit, that enables us to carry out that will: "Now to him who is able to do immeasurably more than all we ask or imagine, *according to his power that is at work within us*" (Eph 3:20, emphasis added).

Further, we learn in Galatians 5:23 that self-control is part of the fruit that the Holy Spirit produces in our lives as we yield to His leading (see 5:19-23).

All of this is why Jesus said to His disciples, speaking on behalf of the triune Godhead, "No branch can bear fruit by itself; it must remain in the vine. Neither can you bear [spiritual] fruit unless you remain in me. I am the vine; you are the branches. If a man remains in me and I in him, he will bear much fruit; apart from me you can do nothing" (Jn 15:4-5).

In short, *God's will and God's power at work in us enable us to break sinful habits.*

That doesn't mean, however, that we somehow become automatons who have no say in the matter, who shift into some kind of holy cruise control until we eventually arrive at Christlikeness. If that were the case, why would the apostle—under the inspiration of the same Holy Spirit who indwells us—urge us to offer our bodies as living sacrifices to God (see Rom 12:1); command us not to think and act like non-Christians anymore (see Rom 12:2); and order us not to use our bodies for sinful purposes or pleasures (see Rom 6:13), among many similar dictates?

These are all biblical commands, which means they're godly things we are to *do*. The Bible, including the New Testament, is full of them. Now, would God command us to do something if we really had no choice in the matter? Of course not. And would He require us to do something knowing we were incapable of complying—in effect, setting us up for failure? Again, the notion is absurd.

Just two verses after Paul told us self-control comes from the Spirit, he wrote, "Since we live by the Spirit, *let us keep in step with the Spirit*" (Gal 5:25, emphasis added). Once more, we see that there's a part for us to play.

In the same vein, the apostle Peter wrote, *"Make every effort* to add to your faith goodness; and to goodness, knowledge; and to knowledge, *self-control*; and to self-control, perseverance; and to perseverance, godliness; and to godliness, brotherly kindness; and to brotherly kindness, love" (2 Pt 1:5-7, emphasis added). Here again, we are called to work at developing Christlike character.

We could go on and on looking at similar scriptures, but the point is clear: While spiritual growth, including the overcoming of sinful habits, is impossible without God, it also requires our willingness and determined effort. We have to work in cooperation with God's Word and Spirit in order to live lives that are pleasing to Him. We cannot think we're somehow going to do it all on our own—especially if we think that by doing so we will earn more of His love—but we also cannot expect to just sit back and wait for God to magically transform us.

*We can trust that God will do His part, and we must do ours as well.* As Saint Augustine said, "Without God, we cannot; without us, God will not."

Let me give an example of how we can cooperate with God in the overcoming of sinful habits. Although I still have a long way to go, I'm gradually improving in my tendency to swear in the car (and elsewhere, truth be told). And in that process, two things are helping greatly.

For one thing, I believe that God works first and foremost through His Spirit and His Word. As I go about my day, if I'm open to His leading, the Spirit will often prompt me to speak or act according to His desires. Most of the time He does that by bringing to mind a passage of Scripture that applies to the situation. The moment I let loose with my tongue, for instance, I'm likely to be reminded of a verse I've memorized, like Psalm 19:14, which says, "May the words of my mouth and the meditation of my heart be pleasing in your sight, O Lord, my Rock and my Redeemer."

As soon as that comes to mind, I'm likely to pray something

like, "Lord, I know the impulse to swear doesn't come from You, and it certainly doesn't please You. Give me the will and the power now to get my temper under control and think and speak in a way that honors You." When I do that, it's amazing how quickly I calm down, get the situation back in a healthy perspective, and bring my tongue under control. (Of course, I may have to repeat this process five minutes later, but the incidents are getting further apart.)

Second, from a Christian book I read several years ago I got the very practical idea of telling my son that I would pay him a dollar each time he caught me swearing. Now, that may not sound too spiritual to some, but I believe it's part of that painful discipline mentioned in Hebrews 12 that God is using to train my unruly tongue. And I can assure you that it has motivated me to think more before I speak, even in a tense situation—and not just when my son is within earshot.

In both cases, God is doing His part by prompting me and offering His provision. When I'm willing to obey, I find the ways and the means to act rightly rather than give in to the impulse to sin.

### Why Do We Struggle So?

The question posed directly above is one that all of us who wrestle with habitual sin ask from time to time. There's no doubt but that the all-powerful God could free us from our addictions instantly and permanently if He chose to do so. In fact, it appears that once in a while He does just that. I've heard any number of people who report that God completely excised some sinful practice from their lives in answer to prayer, and I have no reason to disbelieve them.

So why doesn't He do that for all of us? We would then, among other benefits, have far fewer guilty feelings to deal with. But the undeniable reality is that for most of us, habitual sin and the feelings that go with it are overcome in a process that can seem agonizingly slow, often stopped dead in its tracks, and sometimes even sliding backward.

Why?

I don't think anyone this side of heaven has the complete answer to that question. But let me offer a couple of thoughts for consideration. First, there's the desire to keep control that I mentioned in the preceding chapter. Most of us maintain a part of our lives where we continue in rebellion against God's clear will. *We* want to be in charge. And if we derive some kind of pleasure from our sinful habit, we're not convinced—in spite of all the guilty feelings—that we'll be better off if we cooperate with the Holy Spirit in getting rid of it.

Second, a couple of insightful quotations suggest how God can turn our sinful habits to good. They're both saying essentially the same thing:

"You wonder why God doesn't remove temptation [and your susceptibility to it] from your life? If He did, you might lean on your strength instead of His grace. A few stumbles might be what you need to convince you: His grace is sufficient for your sin."[1]

"Instead of striving for a manmade ticket to heaven based on high achievement and hard work (for which we get all the credit), I suggest we openly declare our own spiritual bankruptcy and accept God's free gift of grace."[2]

In other words, one reason we continue to struggle is that we need to be reminded of how weak we are and of how gracious God is. This doesn't mean He wants us to sin or condones it when we do. Nonetheless, the fact is that every time we fail, we're brought face to face with our need for the Savior, not just once for all eternity but also day by day and even minute by minute. We are humbled. But we exult as well in the assurance that His grace is sufficient, and that as we cooperate with Him, victory is increasingly ours and will one day (in heaven) be complete.

Those are God's promises.

## Grace and Freedom

In John 8:3-11, we have the well-known story of Jesus and the woman caught in adultery. You'll recall that the Pharisees and the teachers of the law brought this woman to Jesus in the hope of finding some grounds on which to condemn Him. They had heard His message of grace, which they perceived (correctly) to be a threat to the legalism they practiced, taught, and sought to impose on everyone else. Now they thought they could get Him to say something contradictory to the Law of Moses, and then they would have their ammunition.

Jesus, knowing their motive, challenged them with His spoken words—"If any one of you is without sin, let him be the first to throw a stone at her" (v. 7)—and with those mysterious words He wrote in the dirt with His finger. None of the men was up to the challenge, and one by one they slipped away.

Finally, only Jesus and the woman were left. "Jesus straightened up and asked her, 'Woman, where are they? Has no one condemned you?'

"'No one, sir,' she said."

Next came Jesus' response of pure, unmerited, priceless grace to a guilty sinner: "'Then neither do I condemn you,' Jesus declared" (vv. 10-11).

That wasn't quite the end of the story, however. The woman now had God's forgiveness (as do we who are in Christ). But what about tomorrow? She had chosen before, at least once, to give in to the temptation to commit adultery. And thanks to Jesus, she had escaped the punishment she deserved. What did He have to say about her future?

His last words to her were at once ennobling, freeing, and, once again, challenging: "Go now and leave your life of sin."

He gave her the dignity, as a child of God, of being responsible for her actions. He gave her the freedom to choose righteousness rather than sin. And He gave her the challenge to make the right choices from that point forward, for the rest of her life.

To you and I, God gives the same dignity, freedom, and challenge.

# The Lasting Consequences of Sin

Half of my patients could go home in a week if they knew they were forgiven.

A DOCTOR WORKING IN A MENTAL HOSPITAL

When I say the name of David, the king of ancient Israel, what descriptive words or phrases come to mind? Perhaps you think of words like *great, powerful, slayer of Goliath, psalmist,* or *man after God's own heart.* But for all his greatness, we can't help thinking as well of his period of greatest sin. By committing several grave offenses with lasting consequences, he gave us a good example of another common reason that God's people feel so guilty so often.

If a man has power on a huge scale, he also has the capacity for evil on a huge scale. The late British historian Lord Acton is not much remembered today except for one statement he wrote in 1887: "Power tends to corrupt and absolute power corrupts absolutely." And David might well qualify as the "poster child" for that famous insight.

As sovereign of Israel, at the height of his power and influence, David could command the life and death of his subjects. Even when his motives were pure evil.

You probably know the story well. (It's recorded in 2 Samuel 11–12.) In the springtime, when his army went out to fight Israel's enemies, David stayed home in Jerusalem. One evening, from the roof of his palace, he saw a beautiful woman bathing. And even though he had a number of wives who could satisfy legitimately his sexual desires, he wanted this new woman.

When he inquired about her, he learned that she, Bathsheba, was the wife of one of his best soldiers. That should have been the end of the story right there, but of course it wasn't. To make a long tale short, David sent for her, committed adultery with her, in the process impregnated her, and then had her husband, Uriah, killed in an attempt to conceal his original crime. After that, he had the audacity to marry the grieving widow!

David didn't realize it at the time, but this series of sins would have consequences for years to come in his personal life, his family life, and the life of his nation.

Those consequences began when David, smugly thinking he had covered his tracks, was confronted by the prophet Nathan, who said on behalf of God,

"Why did you despise the word of the Lord by doing what is evil in his eyes? You struck down Uriah the Hittite with the sword and took his wife to be your own. You killed him with the sword of the Ammonites. Now, therefore, the sword will never depart from your house, because you despised me [God] and took the wife of Uriah the Hittite to be your own." This is what the Lord says: "Out of your own household I am going to bring calamity upon you. Before your very eyes I will take your wives and give them to one who is close to you, and he will lie with your wives in broad daylight. You did it in secret, but I will do this thing in broad daylight before all Israel."

2 SAMUEL 12:9-12

Imagine what David thought and felt as Nathan's prophecies began to come true. One of David's sons, Amnon, raped his sister. Then another of David's sons, Absalom, took revenge by murdering Amnon. Later, Absalom plotted to overthrow and kill David, persuading many in Israel to join his cause (and fulfilling the prophecy about David's wives), but Absalom himself was killed in the attempt. And just two generations after David, a bitter dispute between his heirs led to a permanent split in his once-great kingdom.

Imagine, too, what David thought and felt every time he looked at Bathsheba for the rest of his life. Did he resent her, somehow blaming her for all his misfortune? "If only I'd never seen you that first night..." That would have been a natural—even if unfair—human reaction. Was he uncomfortable in her presence because she reminded him of his sins and stirred deep feelings of guilt?

Beginning with Nathan's challenge and extending through every day thereafter, David was constantly faced with his grievous sins. He simply could not escape the consequences of what he had done. He wrote in Psalm 51, "For I know my transgressions, and my sin is always before me" (v. 3). And it's likely that even though he understood he had been forgiven by God, he struggled with guilty feelings for the remainder of his life.

David is a good example of a simple fact that's as true today as it was in his time: Sin often has results that stay with us for years, perhaps even for the rest of our lives. The results may be physical, emotional, spiritual, or some combination of the three. And they serve as reminders that can bring on fresh waves of guilty feelings every time we encounter them.

A man named Tom, for example, still feels guilty because he married Sarah even though he knew she was not a Christian and he was aware of the biblical instruction to the contrary (see 2 Cor 6:14-15). They've been married for years now. But every time he looks at her, he remembers his willful disobedience and wonders again if God will ever forgive him completely. No amount of confession and repentance has been able to give him the peace of knowing for sure that God accepts him. It doesn't help, either, that Sarah has yet to become a believer. Not surprisingly, there's some heavy tension in their relationship.

Then there's a woman, Elizabeth, who conceived a child out of wedlock years ago. Even though Elizabeth married the child's father, she still feels pangs of guilt every time she looks at her husband or daughter. They serve as constant reminders of her moral failure. *Can God really love someone like me?* she wonders. All the sermons she has heard over the years have not penetrated her heart of hearts and convinced her that He can.

Another man once betrayed a friend in what the man considers to have been a cowardly act. Every time he thought of what he had done, he condemned himself anew. As a result, he developed a contemptuous attitude toward himself that has persisted through the years. He's haunted by guilt because he has never been able to forgive himself, yet he comes across to others as proud. Why? Only by making others feel small is he able to feel any better about himself.[1]

These are just a few examples of a common phenomenon. It's hard to put a past mistake behind us when we get constant reminders of what we did wrong. And when that happens, the burden of guilt can be overwhelming. So we learn to cope in a variety of ways.

## Coping Mechanisms

Because the weight of our guilt can be so heavy, our self-condemnation so severe, we often try to deal with it in some way that "gets around" it—that avoids facing it head-on. My hope is that by exposing these coping mechanisms for what they are, we can begin to lay them aside and choose to do the hard work of dealing directly with our sins and our feelings.

One of the most common ways of avoiding guilt is to stuff it, to try to ignore it. That's called *repression*. Sometimes, for brief periods, we do try to deal honestly with our sins before God. But then, because we still don't feel forgiven, we quickly try to hide from it again. At other times, we repress all thought of our guilt for as long as possible and hope against hope that we'll never have to confront it directly.

We see illustrations of repression in the Bible. David, for example, after Uriah the Hittite had been murdered on his orders, had to have known, in some small corner of his conscience, that what he'd done was terribly wrong. Yet he sent this message to General Joab, who had carried out his order to put Uriah in the front lines of the fiercest fighting against the Ammonites and then abandon him: "Say this to Joab: 'Don't let this upset you; the sword devours one as well as another. Press the attack against the city and destroy it.' Say this to encourage Joab" (2 Sm 11:25).

In other words, "Tell Joab Uriah's death was no big deal.

People die in battle all the time." David's message revealed his total repression of his guilt in the crime.

Then, as if he had buried his conscience along with Uriah, David took Bathsheba for his own wife after her formal period of mourning was over. As far as we can tell, he managed to repress his guilt in the matter until Nathan came along with the shovel of God and exposed the rotting corpse for all to see.

In Luke 18:9, we have a reference to "some who were confident of their own righteousness and looked down on everybody else." They had thoroughly repressed all consciousness of their own sinfulness and guilt before God, convincing themselves in the process that they were morally superior to other people. Jesus felt compelled to tell them a parable showing that God prefers a humble penitent to a self-righteous person, but they all probably thought something like, *I sure hope that sinner over there is listening closely, because he needs to hear this.*

In the book of Proverbs, we have a general principle stated, ironically, by Solomon, David and Bathsheba's second son: "All a man's ways seem right to him, but the Lord weighs the heart" (21:2). We all, like David and those men Jesus confronted, have an amazing capacity to repress the truth about ourselves and justify even our worst behaviors. We can do awful things and yet convince ourselves, even as we're doing them, that our words and actions are good and proper.

As the second part of the verse reveals, however, while we're busily burying the conscious awareness of our guilt, God is watching our every move. There's no deceiving Him.

Another major way we try to get around our guilt is called *projection,* or blame shifting. I do this routinely when I'm alone in my car. If I get angry at a red light and start cursing, it's not my fault. The traffic engineers who can't coordinate the lights properly are to blame. If it's another driver who sets me off, it's his or her fault for being such a thoughtless or even dangerous driver. (I, on the other hand, am a *model* driver.)

But, of course, our guilt projection can get much more serious than that. People who commit crimes regularly blame their parents for doing a bad job of raising them. As I suggested earlier, I wouldn't be at all surprised if David blamed Bathsheba for his downfall: "If she hadn't left her bathroom shade up that night…" And he may well have blamed Uriah for "making" him commit murder: "It's all his fault, really. If he had just slept with his wife that night after I had him brought back from the war, everyone would have thought he was the father of Bathsheba's child, and I wouldn't have needed to kill him to protect my reputation."

Such is the "reasoning" of the human mind when we go into the projection or self-protection mode.

Ultimately, we're tempted to blame God Himself for our failures. We don't give voice to the thoughts, of course, because we're afraid of being irreverent or of how God would react. But if we dared to get brutally honest in our prayers, we would say, "God, You're all-powerful. You could have kept me from doing that if You had wanted to. Why didn't You? When you get down to it, it's all Your fault."

Adam and Eve in the Garden of Eden provide the classic example of this. After they had sinned by eating the forbidden fruit, God asked them rhetorically if that's what they had done. Eve, being less audacious than her husband, projected her guilt only as far as the tempter: "The serpent deceived me, and I ate" (Gn 3:13). It was entirely his fault, not hers.

Adam, however, declared boldly, *"The woman you put here*

*with me*—she gave me some fruit from the tree, and I ate it" (Gn 3:12, emphasis added). In today's English, "God, You're the one to blame here. You put this sinful woman in the garden with me. If You had just left me alone, I never would have listened to that serpent, and I certainly wouldn't have eaten that fruit. I'm a good person."

Most of us fear God too much to be so brazen. Dr. Tournier wrote of us, "Many who do not dare to confess it openly carry hidden within themselves a grudge against God for all their suffering and all their faults.... It is natural for man to project his guilt upon other people and upon God. *But he does not thereby get rid of it*" (emphasis added).[2]

Indeed, even as we blame God, a part of us still knows we're responsible for our own choices, which leads to even more guilty feelings. No guilt-avoidance mechanism is foolproof, either, especially when our sin has had lasting consequences that keep staring us in the face, whether literally or figuratively. And our attempts to use such mechanisms *will* affect those around us.

## An Unwanted Legacy

Earlier in this chapter, I mentioned Elizabeth, the woman who had a child out of wedlock and who feels pangs of guilt every time she sees her daughter or husband (the child's father). But that's not the whole story.

The continual feelings of guilt were unpleasant, to say the least. They made her uncomfortable. As a result, she grew to resent her husband and child. After all, they were the source of her discomfort. They were the reason she had no peace of mind or heart. They were the cause of her inability to forget a transgression that she desperately would have liked to put behind her forever.

Nor did she hide that feeling of resentment or the reason for it. Consequently, her daughter, Melissa, learned to feel guilty about how she was conceived, to feel unwanted and unloved and resentful herself toward her mom and dad.

Without realizing it, and certainly without desiring it, Elizabeth had bequeathed to her daughter an unwanted legacy of bitterness and guilt.

This is just one example of the sad truth that the unresolved guilt we carry around will inevitably affect those closest to us. We may think we have everything under control. We may believe we have completely accepted God's forgiveness of our past sins, been reconciled to those we hurt or who hurt us, and even forgiven ourselves. But if we haven't really dealt with the guilt, we *will* pass it on.

## Before We Forgive Ourselves

If Elizabeth is ever going to forgive herself for conceiving a child out of wedlock, and if Melissa is ever to forgive herself for the way in which she was conceived, what do they need to do? Can they simply choose to do so? Can Elizabeth finally decide that, after all, her sin took place years ago, and she has confessed and repented of it many times? Or can Melissa reach a point of reasoning that she wasn't responsible for the way she came into the world, so there's really no cause for her to feel guilty?

Those approaches sound logical, but there's nothing logical

about our feelings. They don't submit to logic.

No, before Elizabeth can forgive herself, she's going to have to forgive her husband for getting her pregnant in the first place. And Melissa will need to forgive her parents for the sinful way in which her life began, for never fully accepting her, and for projecting their guilt onto her and causing her a great deal of unwarranted misery.

This won't be easy for either woman. It will probably take some time (perhaps a long time) and involve a process of healing rather than happening instantly. And they may well need help, perhaps even professional counseling, to do it. After all, the hurt has been building up for years; and as painful as their lives are, it's the only way of life they know. But until they genuinely forgive those who hurt them and pull out the root of bitterness that has entwined their souls, they will never be able to fully forgive themselves and *feel* forgiven.

A woman named Beverly had a similar experience. In her case, though, she was the one who got pregnant, at age sixteen. Her Christian parents condemned her and, for the nine months leading up to her delivery date, confined her to her bedroom and the upstairs bathroom. They were ashamed of her and would not trust her at all anymore.

Years later, now a married woman, Beverly still could not forgive herself. But she also harbored deep anger toward her parents for the way they had condemned her and kept her under virtual house arrest for those nine months.

Like Melissa, Beverly needed to forgive her parents. Though she had sinned and hurt them badly, they had also sinned and hurt her by responding in an ungracious, unloving manner. Until she resolved that conflict by forgiving them—even if they never asked for it or didn't even think they needed it—she would never be able to forgive herself, either.[3]

Likewise we, if we're struggling to forgive ourselves for some past mistake—especially if it has had lasting consequences—need to look first at whom we need to forgive. It may be parents or other family members, friends, people at work, or others who were connected to the problem in some way. And then, possibly with the help of a wise and caring friend, a pastor, or a counselor, we need to learn how to extend real forgiveness.

In offering forgiveness to others is the key to our own healing.

As we try to do this, however, we should expect opposition that is supernatural in origin. That's the subject we'll explore next.

# eight

# Why a "Guilty" Christian
# May Be Satan's Favorite Kind

The next time the devil reminds you of your past,
remind him of his future.

In *The Hunchback of Notre Dame* (the TNT television version), we have a good picture of what Satan would like to make of every Christian. Monsignor Frodo is, to all outward appearances, a pious, godly man who has devoted his life to the Lord's service. But inwardly, he is actually a tortured, hateful, guilt-ridden wretch.

Frodo has a serious case of lust, and his attentions are centered on the gypsy dancer Esmerelda. He thought he had beaten (literally) the desire for women out of his body years before. And in so doing, he also thought he had earned God's favor. But then he sees Esmerelda for the first time, and in a moment he realizes the desire is still as strong as ever.

How does he respond to this revelation? Does the discovery of his weakness (since, as a priest, he has taken vows of perpetual chastity) drive him to God for comfort or help? Does the reminder that he is a sinner with impure thoughts cause him to throw himself on God's mercy and thank Him for His grace?

No, the effect is quite the opposite. First, he commits murder and a cover-up and then attempts blackmail in an effort to force Esmerelda to submit to his wicked desires. When she resists, his passion for her turns to hatred, he's consumed by guilt, and he tries to deal with both by blaming her for his problems and concluding that she is an evil that must be destroyed.

For Frodo, Esmerelda becomes the embodiment of his own sinful desire. But as Quasimodo the hunchback tells him, "The evil is within you."

Frodo is right where Satan wants him—guilt-ridden, without hope, without joy, and out of fellowship with God. In a word, *defeated*. And that's exactly where Satan wants to put every Christian.

## Our Sworn Enemy

The Bible tells us that Satan is a real being. He was, in fact, one of God's angels, "full of wisdom and perfect in beauty" (Ez 28:12). But he became proud and aspired to take the place of God Himself, so the Lord cast him and the angels who followed him out of heaven (see Is 14:12-15). Altogether, he took one-third of the angels with him (see Rv 12:3-4). They are now the demons who do his bidding.

The book of Revelation tells us that Satan, because of his rebellion against God, is destined to spend eternity in hell. But before he gets thrown into the lake of burning sulfur for good (see Rv 20:10), he wants to make sure he'll be taking as many people with him as he can. To do that, he needs to keep them from hearing the gospel. God uses His people—Christians—to spread the Good News of salvation through faith in Jesus. But if those believers are in a spiritual and emotional condition like Frodo's, how much good news are they going to be spreading?

Thus his determination to keep Christians spiritually defeated, no longer abiding in Christ and so no longer producing fruit (see Jn 15:5).

First Peter 5:8 gives us a graphic word picture of Satan's nature and goal: "Your enemy the devil prowls around like a roaring lion looking for someone to devour." He's a killer, a destroyer. He's powerful, and he's clever. He hates God, and he hates anyone who follows Him. He is God's sworn enemy and ours.

How does he go about causing damage in Christians' lives? He has many methods, enough to fill another book. But one of his most effective is to keep us wallowing in feelings of guilt over past failures, even though we've been forgiven of every sin. He encourages us to think and feel the worst about ourselves, and he encourages others to foster that sense of guilt and shame in us. Psychologist Dr. James Dobson comments, "If we are to be defeated during life's spiritual pilgrimage, it is likely that negative emotions will play a dominant role in that discouragement. Satan is devastatingly effective in using the weapons of guilt, rejection, fear.... Indeed, human beings are vulnerable creatures who could not withstand these satanic pressures without divine assistance."[1]

*If you're still troubled in your soul over something you did in the past, even though you've confessed it to God and repented of any sin that was involved—perhaps many times over—that is Satan's doing, not the Lord's.*

As another writer put it, "If embracing what Christ has done for us doesn't take away the feeling that something is wrong with us, then that feeling is coming from elsewhere [i.e., the devil]."[2]

Satan is the one who wants you to feel like a worm. *He* wants you to think you're a terrible, worthless, no-good person. *He* wants you to believe that your offense, and any others he can dredge out of your memory, "prove" that you're a hopeless sinner.

As for God, "He does not treat us as our sins deserve or repay us according to our iniquities. For as high as the heavens are above the earth, so great is his love for those who fear him; as far as the east is from the west, so far has he removed our transgressions from us" (Ps 103:10-12).

As far as the east is from the west—that's an infinite distance, and that's how far God has removed our guilt from us if we have received His grace offered through Christ (though we may still have to live with the lasting consequences of what we've done). That's the truth of God's Word. So if Satan or one of his minions is invading our thoughts and trying to tell us otherwise, *he's lying,* plain and simple. And he's not doing it for our good or God's.

Lying and deception are what Satan is all about. For example, when he first appeared on earth, in the Garden of Eden, he was full of deceit. In talking with Eve about the forbidden fruit, after she quoted God's warning that eating it would lead to death, Satan told her, "You will not surely die" (Gn 3:4). Talk about your bald-faced lies! He wasn't sneaky in this instance; he directly contradicted God. And he had analyzed Adam and Eve well, because they bought his lie, apparently without hesitation, and committed the first sin.

Jesus pointed to Satan's character when He said of him, "He was a murderer from the beginning, not holding to the truth, for there is no truth in him. When he lies, he speaks his native language, for he is a liar and the father of lies" (Jn 8:44). Just as it is God's nature to speak nothing but the truth, so it is Satan's nature to speak nothing but lies.

That's not to say, however, that he is always so blatant about it as he was in the Garden. He's too clever for that. When it suits his purpose, he (and his demons) can be subtle and cunning. He delights in enticing God's people into thinking they are serving the Lord when they do some evil in His name "for a good cause." A prime example of this would be those who took part in the Spanish Inquisition that began in 1478; while God seeks to draw people to Himself with love, the inquisitors sought to compel people to convert with torture, and they executed them if they did not.

The apostle Paul wrote of Satan's ability to mislead even Christians, "Satan himself masquerades as an angel of light. It is not surprising, then, if his servants masquerade as servants of righteousness. Their end will be what their actions deserve" (2 Cor 11:14-15).

Of course, Satan is not content to bury us in our past failures to keep us mired in guilt. As we see in the account of what happened in the Garden, and in Jesus' own experience (see Mt 4:1-11), Satan and his followers actively work to tempt us, to lead us into making sinful choices. And when we succumb, we have plenty of fresh reason for feeling defeated. So he does all he can to feed our sinful habits, to foster self-centeredness and the multitude of evil desires that grow out of it, like murder, lust, greed, covetousness, and personal ambition.

Even when we resist a temptation, Satan has a way of bringing it right back at us again. Gradually, our strength is worn down, no matter how much we pray. He realizes how discouraging it is for us to be battered by the same enticement over and over.

C.S. Lewis captured this truth when he had his fictional senior demon, Screwtape, write to the junior tempter Wormwood, "You have time itself for your ally.... You see, it is so hard for these creatures [us] to *persevere*. The routine of adversity ... the quiet despair ... of ever overcoming the chronic temptations with which we have again and again defeated them ... all this provides admirable opportunities of wearing out a soul by attrition."[3]

Kurt Stansell, a former Sunday school teacher and church leader, knows all about giving in to temptation and developing what can only be called a sinful addiction. Though a Christian, he was addicted to pornography and topless dance clubs. He would fight the temptation for weeks at a stretch before surrendering once again, seemingly inevitably.

Miserable, and tired of being miserable, Kurt couldn't help wondering why this addiction had so much power over him. He prayed and studied and thought about it, and finally he came to this conclusion: "I began to understand what shame does. When we Christians try to hide something in the darkness, we give Satan incredible license to work in our lives. It's like handing power tools over to him and saying, 'Here, do what you will in my life,' because he's got free rein with all that's hidden when God's light is not shining on it."[4]

Shame over our sin is like a mushroom: It grows best in the dark of a cave, never exposed to the light's revealing rays. And Satan's angels are there with us, whispering in our ear, "You are so bad, and you know it. You'll never be free of this. You're powerless against it. But as bad as you feel now, you'll feel even worse if you say a word about it to anyone, especially God. Think how much you've hurt Him. Think how much you've disappointed Him."

Thus does Satan keep us cowering in the dark. But just in case we don't feel guilty enough about the real sins we commit (or have committed in the past), Satan also works to load us down with *false* guilt.

We didn't make it home for Christmas last year, disappointing our parents, and we feel guilty. We had to say no to the request for help in the church nursery, and we feel guilty. We were too tired to exercise yesterday but not too tired to notice the free donuts in the coffee room, so we conclude we're undisciplined slobs, and we feel guilty. We decided not to follow our parents' example in disciplining our children, and every time they're disobedient we feel guilty. For these and a million other reasons, we can feel we're bad people and bad Christians and find ourselves under a backbreaking burden of guilt, even though our motives may be pure before God.

Once again, Satan is having a field day. As long as our primary spiritual focus is on how guilty we feel, there's no joy or love in our lives to draw a watching world to our Lord.

### The Ultimate Lie

The ultimate lie Satan is trying to sell to Christians—the logical conclusion of all his other lies—is that we're so bad, so guilty, that God won't forgive and accept us anymore, that there are limits to His patience and love, just as there are with many people we've known.

"You've committed this sin just too many times," Satan

whispers. "How can you expect a holy God (yes, he knows God is holy) to accept you when you go on failing in that same area over and over? What kind of Christian does that make you?"

Or his line goes like this: "That sin you committed (hatred, a sexual sin, a lie, divorce, robbery, an abortion, or whatever) is simply too terrible to be forgiven. If other people knew you had done that, they would condemn you, and rightfully so— just as God surely condemns you. Why, you probably aren't really saved at all! Look at how you hurt that other person and how he or she is still suffering today because of it. How can you hope to have that sin forgiven? Think how presumptuous that is! There's no way God can accept you."

As Max Lucado says, "And many believe him [Satan], spending years convinced that they are disqualified from the kingdom."[5]

And so Satan uses our guilt to separate us from our God. The One who gave His very Son to redeem us is feared rather than loved, fled from rather than embraced. The freedom He offers is exchanged for the slavery of guilt and terror.

The Lord weeps, and the devil laughs.

We will look more at how to deal with these feelings of guilt in the next section. But for now let me ask, do you believe— really believe—that God knows everything (*omniscient* is the theological term)? Do you believe the following things from His Word?

O Lord, you have searched me and you know me. You know when I sit and when I rise; you perceive my thoughts from afar. You discern my going out and my lying down; you are familiar with all my ways. *Before a word is on my tongue you know it completely, O Lord....* My frame was not hidden from you when I was made in the secret place. When I was woven together in the depths of the earth, your eyes saw my unformed body. *All the days ordained for me were written in your book before one of them came to be.*

PSALM 139:1-4, 15-16, emphasis added

The fact that God knows everything, including everything we will ever think, say, or do, is one of the central truths of the Bible. Many other passages either state it or demonstrate it. I mention this now, however, to make one simple point: *Nothing* we ever think, say, or do surprises God. Before we were even born, He knew it *all*, including every sin we would ever commit—every lie we would tell; every adulterous thought we would entertain; every murderous intention we would nurture; every selfish and self-serving desire we would indulge; and every good deed we could have done that we chose instead to harden our hearts against. And when we placed our trust in Christ, *He forgave it all.*

Do you really believe it?

This is the truth of God's Word. This is what we say we believe as followers of Jesus. Yet we're so used to living on the basis of our guilty feelings that it's hard to accept His grace and love. Please keep reading, and let's tackle those feelings head-on.

# part two

# Dismantling Our Guilt

# nine

# Gaining a Proper Perspective on God

I think that if God forgives us we must forgive ourselves. Otherwise it is almost like setting up ourselves
as a higher tribunal than Him.

C.S. LEWIS[1]

Chuck Swindoll tells the story of a young woman he met at a conference where he was speaking. She asked to talk with him, and when they sat down together, she told quite a tale.

In years past, she had been sexually promiscuous, she explained. But then, just a couple of years before, she had become a Christian. She was a recipient of God's grace. Yet even now, her feelings condemned her continually for her past sins.

"She was riddled with guilt, overcome with shame," Swindoll writes. "She could hardly maintain eye contact.... Within recent weeks she began to be tortured with shame and the accompanying fear that ... God would judge her."

As Swindoll continued to talk with her, it became clear that she was a true Christian but that she did not understand God's grace. Swindoll opened his Bible to Romans 6 and used it to remind her of God's forgiveness, of her new position in Christ, and of her need to realize that she was no longer a slave to sin. She was free to live for and with God, caught up in His love.

But she resisted, locked in a prison of shame. Satan had her paralyzed with fear. "Time and again she interrupted and reminded me of her past, which intensified her feelings of shame," Swindoll writes. "Her face reflected an inner battle. Her old master didn't want to let her go."

Over and over again, Swindoll repeated the truth of God's Word. She was loved; she was forgiven; she was free. Believe it; accept it; build your life on it. Before he was done, he had described God's grace half a dozen times. "Finally, the light dawned. She forgave herself (a giant step toward accepting grace) and she claimed her freedom."[2]

I take great encouragement from the fact that this woman was so greatly helped, at the level of her feelings, by hearing the truth a number of times in one "session." And I take from it the strategy for this chapter. Namely, from a variety of perspectives, I want to present key truths about our guilt, our God, and our standing in His grace. My prayer is that by the end of the chapter, the light will have dawned for you as well.

### A Forgiving Father

In chapter four, we looked at the story of the Prodigal Son in Luke 15, focusing on the older brother who did not love or forgive his previously sinful sibling. But the key character in that drama, without a doubt, is the father who stands in such stark contrast to that Pharisaic brother. In describing him, Jesus gave us one of our clearest pictures of the nature, the personality, of the living God.

As I've said, part of our difficulty in feeling forgiven is our tendency to think we've done something so terrible that God couldn't possibly forgo judging us for it. But look at what the Prodigal Son did and how his father responded. First, the young man went to Dad and *demanded* to be given his share of the family estate (see v. 12) *now*. Just the way the "request" was made was highly disrespectful; that was the son's first offense.

Consider, too, that a man's estate, then as today, was usually divided among his heirs after his death. So in making his demand, the prodigal was saying, in effect, "I wish you were dead! You're standing in the way of my being able to do what I want." Rather than returning his father's love, he returned venomous spite. That was his second offense, which had to grieve his father's heart deeply, and he hadn't even left home yet.

Now, because this father pictures our heavenly Father, we know he had to have been morally upright and to have taught his sons the same sound values. But what did the young man do? He got his money together, went off to a distant country, and proceeded to violate every moral principle his father had ever espoused. The *New International Version* says the prodigal "squandered his wealth in wild living" (v. 13). *The Living Bible* refers to "parties and prostitutes."

Simply put, the young man indulged in drunkenness, sexual immorality with hookers, and who knows what other kinds of debauchery. He may well have gotten one of his prostitutes pregnant, in which case his response likely would have been to throw some money at her and order her to get out of his sight. Since he was intent on doing everything his father said was wrong, he probably gambled, cursed God, and treated others with arrogant indifference as well. And, of course, he compounded his sins by encouraging others (his fellow party-goers) to follow him down the same path, even paying their way as long as his money held out (which was also as long as their friendship would last).

In short, he repudiated every significant value and standard of his father, not to mention the commandments of God. In effect, he jumped onto his father's sandal-shod feet and spit in his face.

So our list of the prodigal's sins looks like this:

- disrespect for his good and loving father, even wishing him dead

- mockery of God and His holiness

- abandonment of his responsibilities as a son

- materialism and wasteful, self-centered spending

- fornication

- drunkenness

- various additional forms of immorality

- contributing to the corruption of others

- laziness

- and likely still more that I'm overlooking.

That was the pattern of the prodigal. If anyone ever deserved to feel condemned and beyond redemption, it was him. He had earned a prominent place in the sinners' hall of shame.

But then, Jesus said, the young man "came to his senses" and realized he had been going down the "broad ... road that leads to destruction" (Mt 7:13). Face to face with the guilt of his many sins, he made a crucial decision—*one that was the exact opposite of the choice many of us make today.*

Rather than try to hide from his father, as Adam and Eve hid from God in the Garden, or to run from him in terror, the prodigal resolved instead to return to his dad.

And what did he find when he got home?

As we've seen already, he found a bitter, unloving brother. But more importantly, *even before he got there,* he found the warm, accepting, forgiving embrace of a loving father.

"But while he was still a long way off, his father saw him and was filled with compassion for him; he ran to his son, threw his arms around him and kissed him" (Lk 15:20).

Can you picture that scene? While the young man was still trudging down the road—dirty, dusty, and not entirely sure of the welcome he would receive—his father saw him. How did he do that, since the prodigal was still a long way off? *He had climbed to the top of a hill, clambered up the biggest boulder he could find, stretched up to his tallest height, and was eagerly scanning the horizon, hoping desperately that this would be the day his boy came home.*

When at last the father's eyes took in the sight more precious than anything else the world could offer, his heart swelled with love and he jumped down off his perch, gathered the bottom of his robe in his hand so he could move more freely, ran to his son as fast as his legs and his lungs would allow, threw his arms around his child in the biggest bear hug of the century, and kissed him with the joy and passion that only a parent can know—a parent who would gladly give his own life without a moment's hesitation to save his son.

What love! What joy! What complete acceptance!

Now, please listen carefully and understand: That is the exact same welcome God has waiting for us—for *you*—every time you turn to Him, no matter what your sin, no matter what your crime. That's precisely why Jesus told the parable— to give us a clear picture of how our heavenly Father will respond to us when we turn to Him.

Can you picture *that* scene? You know you've failed. You know you've sinned. You're weighed down by guilt. Your guilt has, in turn, developed into shame and self-condemnation. But you know that even being a lowly servant in God's house is better than what you've been going through. So, with fear and trepidation, you finally decide to take a chance, to turn to God and see what will happen.

And what happens? Wow! *The moment you turn in His direction, God is there, waiting to wrap huge, loving arms around you and plant a wet one on your kisser.*

But that's not all. In fact, that's just the beginning.

### The Security of Sonship

As if his incredible greeting weren't enough to warm the prodigal's heart, the father next did something that instantly made his acceptance unmistakable and his son's restoration complete. "The father said to his servants, 'Quick! Bring the best robe and put it on him. Put a ring on his finger and sandals on his feet. Bring the fattened calf and kill it. Let's have a feast and celebrate'" (vv. 22-23).

The passage indicates, as you can see, that the father actually did four things for his child. First, he had the best robe put on him, a long robe of distinction, indicating the wearer was a man of means and importance. Second, he had a signet ring of authority put on the young man's hand; it empowered him to act on the father's behalf and in his name. Third, he had sandals put on his feet, yet another indication of the son's status as a member of the family (slaves went barefoot). Finally, he slaughtered a fattened calf and prepared a feast, signifying that this was a most special occasion.

The son certainly understood the meaning of these actions. But if there were any lingering doubts in his mind about his father's attitude and feelings toward him, they were swept away by what his father next *said:*

"For this son of mine was dead and is alive again; he was lost and is found" (v. 24).

He still called him son! He had regarded him as dead and lost, but never as dismissed from the family; he had never stopped yearning for him as his beloved son. And now that son was alive again and found, so it was time to party!

In the same way, no matter what we've done, God still claims those who are in Christ as His children. We may have been prodigals for a time; we may have done all sorts of things that violate His principles and grieve His heart; we may sometimes act more like sons and daughters of the devil than like the adopted children of the Most High, like those who are spiritually dead rather than like people who have been given new life and freedom. Nevertheless, if we will only turn back to Him, He is eagerly awaiting the opportunity to remind us in unmistakable terms that we are His and He is ours.

*Now and for eternity, we are His beloved children.*

David Seamands, a former missionary to India, tells of a young man named Devadas who thought of himself as a Christian but who had developed a legalistic and joyless faith.

He saw himself as a *servant* of God much more than as a *son.* And in working with Devadas, Seamands came to recognize these key differences between the two mind-sets:

> The servant is accepted and appreciated on the basis of *what he does,* the child on the basis of *who he is.* The servant starts the day *anxious and worried,* wondering if his work will really please his master. The child *rests in the secure love* of his family. The servant is accepted because of his *workmanship,* the son or daughter because of a *relationship....* When a servant fails, his whole position is at stake; he might lose his job. When a child fails, he will be grieved because he has hurt his parents, and he will be corrected and disciplined. But he is not afraid of being thrown out. His basic confidence is in belonging and being loved, and his performance does not change the stability of his position.[3]

Whenever the memory of your past sins starts to make you fear being rejected by God, remember that you are His child, not His servant. Remember, too, the character of your Father.

### The Comfort of God's Character

Looking again at the story of the Prodigal Son, what do we see about the father's character? In his treatment of both sons, we see love, joy, understanding, mercy, forgiveness, patience, warm affection, tenderness, acceptance—in a word, grace. And remember that in describing this father, Jesus was portraying our heavenly Father.

This is the character of our God as He relates to us!

These are the same traits that we can expect Him to demonstrate toward us, even when we're as rebellious as the two sons in Luke 15. Let me quote Romans 8:1 once more: "Therefore, there is now *no* condemnation for those who are in Christ Jesus" (emphasis added). Instead, there is for us God's love, joy, understanding, mercy, forgiveness, patience, warm affection, tenderness, acceptance—in a word, yes, grace.

If we're ever going to feel as completely forgiven by God as we are in fact, we must come to know *and believe* these truths about His character. His wrath is reserved for those who have rejected His Son, not for those who have become His adopted children. We have no reason to flee Him in fear, but every reason to embrace Him in love and gratitude.

"Taste and see that the LORD is *good;* blessed is the man who takes refuge in him," David wrote in the Psalms (34:8, emphasis added). David also wrote, "You [God] will show me the path of life; in Your presence is fullness of joy; at Your right hand are pleasures forevermore" (Ps 16:11, NKJV).

Similarly, the prophet Jeremiah told us in the book of Lamentations, "Because of the LORD'S great love we are not consumed, for *his compassions never fail. They are new every morning;* great is your faithfulness" (3:22-23, emphasis added).

In short, God wants to bless us. His mercies pour down upon us every day. And the closer we get to Him, the more lasting, overflowing joy we will find.

To illustrate God's gracious character, Chuck Swindoll recounts the story of David and Mephibosheth, the sole remaining child of David's closer-than-a-brother friend, Jonathan. Once he became king, David wanted to show kindness to the descendants of his deceased friend. Mephibosheth, who had been permanently crippled as a child, was the only one left.

Now, understand that as Jonathan's son and King Saul's grandson, Mephibosheth could have become a potential rival to David for the throne of Israel. Many kings in David's place would have executed such a person without a moment's hesitation. But David instead had him brought from the obscure little town of Lo Debar into the royal palace, where he treated Mephibosheth like one of his own sons. (You can read the whole story in 2 Samuel 9.)

Swindoll writes of that incident, and of how God has likewise shown kindness to us:

> David restored Mephibosheth from a place of barrenness to a place of honor. He took this broken, handicapped person from a hiding place where there was no pastureland and brought him to the place of plenty, right into the very courtroom of the king. The analogy is clear. God has taken us from where we were and brought us to where he is—to a place of fellowship with him. He has restored us to what we once had in Adam.[4]

That's the kind of God we have, and the kind of love He has for us. Such love inspired the apostle Paul to write the famous, fabulous words of Romans 8:38-39: "For I am convinced that neither death nor life, neither angels nor demons, neither the present nor the future, nor any powers, neither height nor depth, nor anything else in all creation, will be able to separate us from the love of God that is in Christ Jesus our Lord."

That incredible love also inspired Steve Thurman, my former pastor, to write concerning Paul's declaration, "Let that sink in for a moment. Paul is *convinced*, he is certain, he is persuaded, that absolutely *nothing* can separate the Christian from the love of God. How we live or die, what choices we make today or tomorrow, *nothing* can cut us off from God's affection. No matter what the failures of our lives, no matter how severe and continuous our sins may be, God's love for us continues to be … *relentless*."[5]

Indeed, let that sink in. The relentless love of God will never let you go. It will *never* give up on you. It will *never* desert you. It will *never* reject you. No matter how often you fail; no matter how egregious your sin; God's love remains constant.

"Is there any reason to think," writes Max Lucado, "that the One who received you the first time won't receive you every time?"[6] And the answer is a resounding no. That's the nature, the character, of our heavenly Father.

# Trusting in God's Purposes

*Am I in the place of God? You intended to harm me,*
*but God intended it for good to accomplish what is*
*now being done, the saving of many lives.*

JOSEPH, IN GENESIS 50:19-20

When we first looked in chapter four at the story of the Prodigal Son, we focused on the judgmental older brother. But the prodigal himself has a thing or two to teach us about how to feel forgiven.

When he came to his senses in the far country of sin and returned to his father, he was met by his dad's compassionate bear hug. Then the young man said the words he had resolved to say back in the pigsty of spiritual poverty: "Father, I have sinned against heaven and against you. I am no longer worthy to be called your son" (Lk 15:21).

With that brief statement, the no-longer-prodigal brought his sin into the open and made confession. In so doing, he let his father know that he was truly home—spiritually and not just physically. In that moment, with those few words, he revealed himself to be more of a son—more like his father—than he (or his older brother) had ever been before. And, recognizing this, his father restored him to that relationship.

Because of the shame we so often feel and which Satan so effectively exploits, as we saw in chapter eight, we tend to try to hide our sins, even from God. That's not logical, of course; it's driven by our guilty fear of God. But as we see in the parable and in everyday experience, when we instead bring our failures into the open and get honest with God, *that's* when we find freedom from guilt and the restoration of our relationship with Him.

After all, how can God offer grace and His loving embrace when we're still denying we need them?

In Psalm 32, David captured beautifully both the burden we bear when we try to hide sin and the freedom we feel when we bring it into the open. "When I kept it all inside," he wrote, "my bones turned to powder, my words became daylong groans. The pressure never let up; all the juices of my life dried up. Then I let it all out; I said, 'I'll make a clean breast of my failures to God.' Suddenly the pressure was gone—my guilt dissolved, my sin disappeared" (vv. 3-5, THE MESSAGE). David's openness before God brought relief and, even more, a renewed appreciation of God's mercy and forgiveness.

As Kurt Stansell, the man from chapter eight who had been bound by sexual addiction and shame, put it, "I learned that the more open I could be, the less of a hold Satan seemed to have."[1] In his case, that meant first getting honest with God. Then he also revealed his addiction to his pastor, to his church men's group, and finally, after much prayer and preparation, to his wife.

Several times in this book, I've referred almost in passing to 1 John 1:9, a well-known verse about God's forgiveness. But now let me turn the spotlight on it for a moment: *"If we confess our sins,* he is faithful and just and will forgive us our sins and purify us from all unrighteousness" (emphasis added). Note the part emphasized. The process of being restored to God's fellowship after we've failed, like a prodigal child, and of enjoying His embrace *and knowing in our deepest heart that we are forgiven and accepted* begins with bringing our sins into the open before Him in humble yet expectant prayer.

In addition, we will only be able to forgive *ourselves* when we're this honest about what we've done. "There must be truthfulness. Without honesty, self-forgiveness is psychological hocus-pocus. The rule is: we cannot really forgive ourselves unless we look at the failure in our past and call it by its right name."[2]

Openness with God, then, is essential to feeling forgiven. In the past, however, that has been a terrifying prospect for many of us. That's why I discuss it only after the reminder in the preceding chapter of God's forgiving nature, our security as His children, and His good and loving character.

The bottom line: If we'll pause to think about it in the light of God's truth, we have no reason to hide from Him, regardless of how or how often we've sinned, and every reason to come to Him in honest confession and repentance. We can return to our Father to bare our souls again and again—as often as necessary—knowing we *will* find compassion, understanding, and forgiveness.

We also have the consolation of knowing that God often uses even the bad we do to help bring about His good purposes.

## The Consolation of God's Purposes

When the Prodigal Son went to his father and asked for his share of the estate, he was in rebellion. Determined to taste the sinful pleasures of the world, he had already rejected his dad and his dad's values. Was there any way the father, by refusing the young man's request and trying to keep him at home, could have forced his son to his senses and restored him to fellowship?

No. By "locking him up and throwing away the key," Dad would have only driven Junior deeper into rebellion. So, as painful as it was to let his son go and to contemplate the sinfulness on which the young man was intent, it was in reality the father's only hope of one day getting his child back as a true son and a willing follower of God. And only by putting his own values to the test would the young man eventually see how bankrupt they were and how right his dad had been all along.

The son *wanted* to leave out of sinful desire and rebellion. The father *let* him leave, difficult though it was, as a way of accomplishing *his* purpose.

One of the best-known and most comforting verses in the Bible is Romans 8:28: "And we know that in all things God works for the good of those who love him, who have been called according to his purpose." We've heard it, we believe it, and in difficult times we cling to it. But can we believe it also applies to our failures? Can we believe that even though our sins themselves are bad, God can bring good out of them?

I take great hope in the truth expressed by David in Psalm 103: "As a father has compassion on his children, so the Lord has compassion on those who fear him; for he knows how we are formed, he remembers that we are dust" (vv. 13-14). God knows the stuff we're made of—He made us. And He remembers that we're just dust—weak, insubstantial, prone to crumbling under the pressure of temptation, even though He has made it possible for us to endure (see 1 Cor 10:13).

*In other words, God has a more realistic view of us than we have of ourselves.*

We tend to think, spurred on by the whispered accusations of the devil, that if we fail, we've blown it for good and God no longer loves and accepts us. But God knows that we're bound to fail apart from Him. No sin of ours ever takes Him by surprise. He realized when He made us that we would fail many times and in grievous ways, and that as a result we would need a Savior. That's why He sent His Son, so that whosoever will may come.

This does not excuse our sins or make us any less respon-sible, but it does mean that God is bigger than our failures and is able to make good come out of even them. In fact, I suspect that God uses us *in spite of ourselves* far more often than He is able to use us because we are "in step with the Spirit" (Gal 5:25).

I like the way Dr. Tournier put the matter: "God's plan of salvation is not only accomplished by men's obedience, but even through their resistances and disobediences. This is the answer to all those people who cannot forgive themselves for their past faults.... Fulfillment of God's plan is happily not dependent upon the faultless obedience of men!... What is amazing is that He ... uses their faults and their hardness of heart."[3]

Could God use David's hardness of heart toward Uriah the

Hittite—the man David sent to his death so he (David) could take his wife—to accomplish His good purposes? Indeed! We won't know all the ways He did that until we get to heaven, but some of the more obvious ways center on the person of Solomon.

The first child born to David and Bathsheba, the child conceived in sin, died in infancy. Their second child was Solomon, whom God used to bless Israel and the rest of the world both in his lifetime and for all eternity. How? For one thing, Solomon would prove to be Israel's greatest king. He expanded her territory, her wealth, and her reputation to the greatest extent she would ever know. His reign was the highwater mark of the kingdom's entire history.

Solomon also blessed Israel and the world spiritually. First, God used him to build His temple in Jerusalem, His first permanent dwelling place among humankind. Second, Solomon's own life, as recorded in Scripture, teaches us many valuable lessons both positive and negative about living for God. And third, the Lord inspired Solomon to write many passages that themselves became a part of the Bible (e.g., the Song of Solomon, Ecclesiastes, and much of Proverbs).

Finally and most importantly, Solomon became part of the human family line that would eventually lead to the birth of God's Savior, Jesus the Christ (see Mt 1:1-16). Talk about redeeming a sin-laden tragedy!

Another prime biblical example of human sin being turned to good by a gracious God is the story of the birth and early years of Moses in the book of Exodus. You'll recall that the Hebrew patriarch Jacob had brought his family to Egypt in order to survive a terrible famine and to be reunited with his beloved son Joseph, who had become the pharaoh's prime minister. After they had settled there, the family grew over the years into the nation of Israel, with upwards of a million people.

During that same period, after Joseph's death, his memory and Egypt's gratitude for all the good he had done gradually faded. Eventually a pharaoh ascended the throne "who did not know about Joseph" (Ex 1:8). What he *did* know was that the people of Israel had grown so numerous that they could become a dangerous enemy if they ever turned against Egypt. So he turned them into slave laborers, leading them to cry out to God for deliverance. Then the pharaoh pragmatically but ruthlessly issued an order that all the male babies born to Hebrew mothers should be killed.

This was pure evil directed at the most innocent of people. The idea was undoubtedly inspired by Satan, the destroyer.

But God had another idea.

He gave the Hebrew midwives who helped deliver the babies the courage to ignore pharaoh's order. And so one day a boy was born whom his parents named Moses. Under normal circumstances, they would have cared for him in their home and raised him to be a nice, normal Hebrew man. The situation in which they lived, however, was anything but normal.

They hid Moses from the murderous Egyptians for three months. Then, when they could hide him no longer, his mother put him in a basket and set him afloat on the Nile. There he was soon found and adopted by the pharaoh's daughter. She, in turn, unwittingly hired his own real mother to nurse him and rear him until she was ready to take him into her palace and make him into an Egyptian prince.

Thus did God use the pharaoh's bloodthirsty command to

save and to begin the preparation of His appointed deliverer, who would one day lead Israel out of bondage and back to the land of promise.

The ultimate biblical example of God's bringing good from evil is, of course, the event that took place on Calvary's hill two thousand years ago. Christ's crucifixion was at the same time both the greatest crime in human history and the supreme demonstration of God's love for human beings. Satan, inspiring Jesus' betrayer and executioners, saw it as his moment of triumph—his opportunity to kill the Son of God, who had made Himself vulnerable by humbly becoming a man. But God knew it was *His* moment of triumph, the ultimate act of self-sacrifice by which He would make possible the redemption of His fallen creatures—and then demonstrate His power over death and victory over the devil by raising His Son to life again on the third day.

Knowing that God works this way—that Romans 8:28 is true in all cases—puts our failures and our feelings in a different light, doesn't it? When we sin, we need to confess it and receive His cleansing (see 1 Jn 1:9). But then we can move on with our lives, knowing we didn't take God by surprise, and that we're not only (first and foremost) forgiven, but also that He can and will turn it to good in some way. Or as Chuck Swindoll says, "Our imperfect state keeps us from ever forgetting that where sin abounds, grace *super*abounds."[4] I find great hope in that reality.

Further, knowing that God works to bring good from our failures, we can look for ways to cooperate with Him. Counselor, speaker, and author Gary Smalley explains, "Avoid the blame game. Don't beat yourself up over mistakes you've made.... If you can avoid shame and blame, your recovery will be much quicker. Try to say, 'Okay, this happened to me, now what can I do to make it better?' or 'What new opportunities does this open up for me?' Try to ask yourself the question 'How am I becoming a better or more loving person because of this event?'"[5]

Thinking back, for example, to the incident described in chapter one where I lost my temper with my young son, I know God used it to help make me a more patient, tender, self-controlled father. The memory of that night, while painful, nonetheless prodded me to work with His help at becoming a better dad. And when I lose my cool in the car while driving alone, any temptation to pride that I might be feeling is instantly blown away. Again, I'm not trying to excuse my sin, but this understanding of how God works does help to keep my shortcomings in perspective and stop me from wallowing in unnecessary and, yes, ungodly feelings of guilt.

### A Bill Already Paid

Another step in dealing with our guilty feelings is to anchor in our souls the truth that we could never earn God's forgiveness but that—praise be to God!—we don't have to because Jesus already did. Although we have a hard time accepting this, the central truth of biblical Christianity is that we could *not* save ourselves, and that God, knowing this, sent His Son to pay the penalty for sin that we deserved so we could enjoy the relationship with Him that we did not deserve.

Perhaps these words from Chuck Swindoll will help to plant this truth deep in our hearts: "[Grace] is absolutely and totally free. You will never be asked to pay it back. You couldn't even if you tried. Most of us have trouble with that thought, because we work for everything we get. As the old saying goes, 'There ain't no free lunch.' But in this case, grace comes to us free and clear, no strings attached. We should not even try to repay it; to do so is insulting."[6]

In Romans 12:2, the apostle Paul instructed us, "Do not conform any longer to the pattern of this world, but *be transformed by the renewing of your mind.* Then you will be able to test and approve what God's will is—his good, pleasing and perfect will" (emphasis added). And the issue before us now is one of the key areas in which we need to have our minds renewed by the truth of God's Word.

When you think about it, there are really only two major religions in the world, and the question of how we get right with God is what distinguishes between them. Biblical Christianity says that we could never earn the forgiveness of a holy God, but that that's OK because He provided a Savior for us, Jesus Christ. Faith in Him is what gives us the forgiveness of our sins and adoption into God's family. Salvation is a free *gift* of God's grace. It cost God everything; it costs us nothing.

All other religions, on the other hand, claim that in some way or other, we can and must earn our way into heaven (however they conceive of it). Our good works or obedience to some code of conduct are the determining factor in our eternal destiny. Our performance is the key.

The contrast between the two faiths could not be more stark. Either we depend on the finished work of Jesus Christ on the cross on our behalf or we depend on our own goodness. The central question of human existence is this: What will you do with Jesus Christ? Was He only a good man and maybe even a prophet of God, or is He the risen, living Son of God and your personal Savior?

If He is the latter to you, then please believe His words when He said, just before He died on Calvary's cross, "It is finished" (Jn 19:30). His work of redeeming us *is* finished. The penalty for our sins *has been* paid. No matter what we do now or how often we do it—no matter how bad our sins seem to us—the price *has already been paid in full* by the Son of God. There's nothing left to pay.

Imagine that you go out for dinner to the best restaurant in your town. You order the most expensive appetizer, the most expensive entrée, the most expensive dessert. You also have a couple of beverages and then coffee with your dessert. As the end of the evening approaches, you know you've run up quite a bill. In fact, you got a little carried away, and you realize you don't have nearly enough money to pay it, and your credit cards are already maxed out. You begin to dread the moment when the waiter will present you with the check.

That moment soon arrives, however, and as the waiter approaches with the leather-covered tally of your debt in his hand and a smile on his face, you break into a cold sweat. What will you do? You can't possibly pay your bill. You're in trouble.

Accepting the check with one hand, with your other you loosen your collar and take a big gulp of air. As you open the cover, you close your eyes, terrified of what you're going to see. Then, slowly, one at a time, you open your eyes to see … a balance owed of zero! Stamped in red block letters across the bill are the words PAID IN FULL.

You can't believe your eyes. For a minute you're dumbstruck, your mouth hanging open. Finally you turn to the smiling waiter. "I don't understand," you tell him. "What's going on?"

"Someone who apparently cares for you very much has paid your bill," he says. "Isn't that wonderful? Have a pleasant evening."

"But this can't be," you insist. "I have to pay it."

"Well, to be perfectly honest," the waiter says, "when your friend paid the bill for you, he said he was quite sure you *couldn't* pay it."

"But I just know you won't consider this bill paid unless *I* pay it. You've *got* to let me pay it," you demand.

"But Sir, the bill has already been paid in full. It's done. There is nothing left for you to pay. You're free to go on and enjoy the rest of your life."

"No, no, no!" you persist. "*I've* got to pay it. I don't know how I can, but I know I must."

Shaking his head in sad disbelief, the waiter turns and walks away.

That's an unbelievable story, isn't it? You'd be a fool to go on insisting like that when your bill had already been covered by a generous friend. And yet that's exactly what we often do with regard to God's forgiveness. Our sin debt was paid in full some two thousand years ago, yet we go on demanding that we have to pay it, even though we never could.

Can you see how futile it is to continue trying to earn God's salvation? Can you see how great and marvelous is His grace toward you? As you reflect on it, can you let this wonderful truth begin to reach you at the level of your feelings?

## Living Beyond the Level of Feelings

Ultimately, dealing with our guilty feelings in a healthy way comes down to what we saw in chapter three: We have to recognize that our feelings, our emotions, are a very poor measure of what's true and right. And we have to choose to act according to what we know to be God's truth rather than go on allowing our feelings to dominate our lives.

Satan is constantly at work against us, whispering accusations in our ears, stirring up the guilty feelings that come so easily. The words of C.S. Lewis are directly to the point here:

Remember what St. John says: "If our *heart* condemn us, God is stronger than our heart." The *feeling* of being, or not being, forgiven and loved, is not what matters. One must come down to brass tacks. If there is a particular sin on your conscience, repent and confess it. If there isn't, tell the despondent devil not to be silly. You can't help *hearing* his voice (the odious inner radio) but you must treat it merely like a buzzing in your ears or any other irrational nuisance.[7]

The same counsel applies if what comes to mind is a sin that we've already confessed and repented of. If we've done those things, remember that 1 John 1:9 says God has been faithful to forgive and cleanse us of it—*so He isn't the one bringing that sin back to mind.* We need to thank Him for His grace, ask for His strength to live like the restored prodigal children of His that we are, and move on.

The passage to which Lewis referred above is also found in 1 John: "This then is how we know that we belong to the truth, and how we set our hearts at rest in his [God's] presence whenever our hearts condemn us. For God is greater than our hearts, and he knows everything" (3:19-20). If we find our hearts—our feelings—condemning us, the apostle said, we must submit them to His truth. Are we dealing with true guilt over a true violation of God's will, in which case 1 John 1:9 is our proper response? Or is Satan or a hyperactive conscience at work, in which case we need to get past our feelings and rest in Jesus' finished work and the Father's unfailing love?

At the beginning of his second letter to the young evangelist Timothy, the apostle Paul sought to encourage him to be faithful to God in difficult times, when it's easy to be afraid and carried away by feelings. Note the way Paul did that: "For God has not given us a spirit of fear, but of power and of love and of a *sound mind*.... I *know* whom I have believed and *am persuaded*.... *Hold fast* the pattern of sound words which you have heard from me, in faith and love which are in Christ Jesus" (2 Tm 1:7, 12, 13, NKJV, emphasis added).

All through the passage, Paul was exhorting his son in the faith to think clearly, to remember whose Word he was trusting, to hang on to the truth. This, Paul insisted, was the antidote to feelings that threatened to mislead and to derail the work of God in Timothy's life. And this is still our proper response today.

Mind you, I don't mean to suggest this is easy. If we've been struggling with guilt for years, we can and should first pray for God's help to see the truth and believe His Word. In some cases, that alone will bring an immediate and enduring feeling of freedom from condemnation. But many more of us will need to grow into that feeling over a period of time, as our minds are steadily transformed and renewed by the truth (remember Romans 12:2). We will fall back into despair occasionally. But by God's grace, we can increasingly be of sound mind; we can *know* and *be convinced* and *hold fast* to the truth that we are the loved, forgiven, and fully restored children of a great and good Father God.

One practical way we can foster the renewing of our minds is by memorizing scriptures that remind us of essential truths. Then, when the guilty feelings return, we can counter them with God's Word—just as Jesus countered Satan's temptations in the wilderness—and be reassured of our forgiveness and acceptance by the Father. Many of the passages we've looked at in this book are appropriate for this purpose.

I strongly encourage you to write them down on cards to carry with you as you memorize them and put them to work in your life. With a little effort, anyone can learn a verse or two each week; Scripture memorization isn't just for the young. And the Holy Spirit *will* bring these nuggets of God's truth and promises to mind when we need them.

Here are a few verses to get you started in this mind-renewing process:

Therefore, there is now no condemnation for those who are in Christ Jesus.

ROMANS 8:1

Who will bring any charge against those whom God has chosen? It is God who justifies. Who is he that condemns? Christ Jesus, who died—more than that, who was raised to life—is at the right hand of God and is also interceding for us. Who shall separate us from the love of Christ?

ROMANS 8:33-35

For God was in Christ,... no longer counting men's sins against them but blotting them out. This is the wonderful message.

2 CORINTHIANS 5:19, TLB

Christ died for the ungodly.... Since we have now been justified by his blood, how much more shall we be saved from God's wrath through him! ... Not only is this so, but we also rejoice in God through our Lord Jesus Christ, through whom we have now received reconciliation.

ROMANS 5:6, 9, 11

For Christ died for sins once for all, the righteous for the unrighteous, to bring you to God.

1 PETER 3:18

If we confess our sins, he is faithful and just and will forgive us our sins and purify us from all unrighteousness.

1 JOHN 1:9

He does not treat us as our sins deserve or repay us according to our iniquities. For as high as the heavens are above the earth, so great is his love for those who fear him; as far as the east is from the west, so far has he removed our transgressions from us.

PSALM 103:10-12

But you were washed, you were sanctified, you were justified in the name of the Lord Jesus Christ and by the Spirit of our God.

1 CORINTHIANS 6:11

But you are a chosen people, a royal priesthood ... that you may declare the praises of him who called you out of darkness into his wonderful light.... Once you had not received mercy, but now you have received mercy.

1 PETER 2:9-10

For being saved is a gift; if a person could earn it by being good, then it wouldn't be free—but it is! It is given to those who do not work for it. For God declares sinners to be good in his sight if they have faith in Christ to save them from God's wrath. King David spoke of this, describing the happiness of an undeserving sinner who is declared "not guilty" by God. "Blessed, and to be envied," he said, "are those whose sins are forgiven and put out of sight. Yes, what joy there is for anyone whose sins are no longer counted against him by the Lord."

ROMANS 4:4-8, TLB

As we first memorize such verses and then review them from time to time, they will take deep root in our minds and our thoughts. There, the Holy Spirit will use them to transform us, to change our feelings, and to give us the kind of security in our relationship with our heavenly Father that the prodigal enjoyed in his sonship after he returned to his loving father.

For example, when I'm tempted to feel shame over sins I've already confessed, I like to contemplate the imagery of Psalm 103. The idea that my guilt has been removed from me as far as the east is from the west—just how far is infinity, anyway?—is extremely appealing. My guilt truly is *gone*.

## Is God Good?

How do we who have placed our faith in Jesus Christ deal with those nagging guilty feelings even after we've confessed and repented of our sins? We recall and dwell on these things:

- God's forgiving nature

- the relationship of being His children into which He has brought us

- His loving, accepting character

- the freedom we have to be open with God about our shortcomings

- the way He uses even our failures to accomplish His purposes

- the central fact of our faith—that Jesus has already paid our sin debt in full

- the reality that because our feelings are a poor gauge of truth, they must not dominate our thoughts and actions but be subordinate to God's Word.

In the end, all this boils down to the way we answer one crucial question: Is God really good? Put another way, Is He for us or against us? Does He seek what's best for us, or does He seek to condemn and destroy us?

In their heart of hearts, many Christians believe that God is *not* good, that Romans 8:1 is not true, at least for them. That is a lie straight from the pit of hell, the same lie Satan has been telling people since the Garden of Eden. It's why we continue to fear God when we have every reason to be thanking Him, praising Him, and running into His loving, welcoming embrace.

If we will take God at His word and begin to focus instead on how deep and broad and high and vast is His love for His children, we will be amazed. We will be overcome by His grace. And we will fall to our knees in praise and adoration of our loving Lord.

# The Difference Between Forgiving and Forgetting

Since God has dumped your sins into the sea, do you want to throw them a life preserver?

JOHN NIEDER AND THOMAS THOMPSON[1]

When I was about six or seven years old, I committed a crime for the first and, I think, only time in my life.

One day while my parents and siblings and I were visiting close family friends, I went exploring through their big farmhouse. When I found my way to the master bedroom, I discovered a wondrous thing in the eyes of a small boy—a tray covered with all kinds of loose change. Out of youthful impetuosity, yet knowing it was wrong, I scooped up a handful of coins and put them in my pocket.

As my family began to drive home that evening, my crime was discovered. I don't remember now how it happened, but I'm sure I wasn't a clever thief. In any event, we turned around and went back to our friends' house, and there I was made to turn in the money and offer an apology.

Our friends were more amused than shocked; to them it was no big deal, and I wouldn't be surprised if they've forgotten it completely. I, on the other hand, have never forgotten.

Though I realize it was a very minor offense in the annals of human crime, I still feel a twinge of guilt on those rare occasions when the event comes back to mind. I like to think of myself as an honest, trustworthy person who doesn't even take a paper clip that doesn't belong to him, but that memory reminds me that there's at least a little shameful larceny in my soul after all.

All of this raises a crucial question: If I still remember the incident after more than thirty years, and if I still feel even a little guilt about it, have I ever really forgiven myself?

There's a certain kind of logic, common among Christians, that would say I haven't. If I had, this line of reasoning goes, I should have been able to put the matter behind me completely and never be bothered by it again. Conversely, since I've never forgotten it, I must never have forgiven myself. And as we've seen, in our feelings-dominated culture, if I don't *feel* forgiven, I'm likely to think that maybe God can't totally forgive me, either.

Thus, our inability to wipe our sins from our minds is easily taken as evidence that we're not really, fully forgiven no matter how many times we've confessed and repented, and our feelings of guilt are compounded.

## Doesn't God Forget?

Our tendency to think this way is reinforced, ironically, by our awareness of Bible verses that say God does forget our sins. He said in Jeremiah 31:34, for example, "For I will forgive their wickedness and will remember their sins no more." In Isaiah 43:25 He said, "I, even I, am he who blots out your transgressions, for my own sake, and remembers your sins no more." As we've seen, David wrote of God in Psalm 103:12, "As far as the east is from the west, so far has he removed our transgressions from us."

In the New Testament, the apostle Peter, in one of the first sermons given in the early days of the church, said, "Repent, then, and turn to God, so that your sins may be wiped out, that times of refreshing may come from the Lord" (Acts 3:19).

From these and similar passages, we conclude that this is the way forgiveness is supposed to work in our lives as well. After all, aren't we meant to emulate God? Isn't His example the ideal? So true, complete forgiveness (of ourselves in the context of this book) must include not only making things right with God, but also forgetting the offense, wiping it from our minds as if it had never happened.

Such thinking, however, is simply wrong and unrealistic. There are two basic flaws with it: First, we aren't God; and second, we're misunderstanding what Scripture means when it says that God forgets our offenses.

About the first flaw, I would hope I don't need to say much. (Of course, as the second half of Romans 1 explains, human beings are constantly trying to play God.) But clearly, we are not deity. God is all-knowing; we, by comparison, have the understanding of a fence post. He is all-powerful; we are pathetically weak. He makes all things work together for His purposes in ways we can't begin to comprehend; only by His grace can we do anything of eternal value.

Thus, just because God can do something is no reason to assume that we can also do it, or that we can do it as well as He can if He, in love, has given us some ability in a given area.

Regarding the second flaw in our reasoning, we need to look carefully at what the Bible means when it says God forgets. Does it mean, as we seem to suppose, that He develops some sort of selective amnesia about our sinfulness? When we state the assumption "out loud" or read it in black and white, it doesn't make much sense, does it? How could the all-knowing One, He who sees the past as well as the present and future with perfect objectivity, somehow delete all awareness of the sins of His people—a significant chunk of human history—from His memory banks?

So what does the Bible mean when it says that God forgets our sins? It means that He forever and completely removes the guilt of our sins from us. "As far as the east is from the west," Psalm 103 says. It means He won't hold our sins against us anymore. The guilt we bore was taken from us and placed on the shoulders of Jesus Christ at Calvary. The penalty we deserved was paid in full. God has only love and compassion for us now—no judgment, no condemnation.

Lewis Smedes put it this way: "True, the Bible says that God promises to forgive us *and* forget.... But does he forget the way we forget when we can't remember where we put our keys? Of course not.... [T]o say that God forgets is to say that he *feels* about us the way he *would* feel if he *had* forgotten."[2]

To forgive ourselves, then, is not to forget what we did wrong; that's impossible. Rather, it is to let what God has removed (our guilt) stay removed from us. It means not holding our sin against ourselves but accepting His grace with grateful hearts instead of insisting to Him, "You can't be serious!"

Indeed, not only is forgetting our sins impossible, but even if we could do it, it would be a bad idea.

## The Importance of Remembering

Contrary to what we often think, it's important that we remember our sins in a healthy way even after we accept God's forgiveness. Why? First, because only by remembering can we learn from our mistakes.

When am I apt to lose my temper, profane God's name, and hurt others or myself in the process? What conditions, both external and internal, make me vulnerable to the temptation? Only by examining my past failures do I gain that knowledge. And only with that knowledge can I take precautions in the future to avoid the loss of self-control, or to regain it sooner rather than later when I start to slip.

In 1 Corinthians 10, Paul tells us that the sins of the Jews recorded in the Old Testament "occurred as examples to keep us from setting our hearts on evil things as they did" (v. 6). In other words, the account of their sins was written down for all time so that we, believers through the ages, might learn from their mistakes. Then Paul warns, "So, if you think you are standing firm, be careful that you don't fall!" (v. 12).

In John 8, which we first explored in chapter six, when Jesus told the woman caught in adultery that her sins were forgiven, did He then tell her to try to forget what she had done? No. He told her, "Go now and leave your life of sin." In other words, knowing full well what she had been and done in the past, she was now to choose instead—every day for the rest of her life—to live like a forgiven child of her heavenly Father. She was to take care that she never again would fall into the sin of adultery.

Likewise, by recalling our own offenses, we're reminded of how weak we are, we're kept humble, and we're warned to avoid or at least prepare for (mentally, emotionally, spiritually) those situations and circumstances that we know will tempt us to fail once more.

Second, it's vital that we remember our faults because only then can we do the real work of forgiving ourselves. Only by bringing things into the open can we deal with them. Conversely, if we try to forget, to bury the painful memories in the hidden recesses of our minds, we do not resolve our guilt and we set ourselves up for still more pain in the future.

"If you forget, you will not forgive at all," Lewis Smedes explains. He continues:

> You can never forgive people [including yourself] for things you have forgotten about. You need to forgive precisely because you have not forgotten what someone did; your memory keeps the pain alive long after the actual hurt has stopped.... Forgetting, in fact, may be a dangerous way to escape the inner surgery of the heart that we call forgiving.... The pains we dare not remember are the most dangerous pains of all. We fear to face some horrible thing that once hurt us, and we stuff it into the black holes of our unconsciousness where we suppose it cannot hurt us. But it only comes back disguised; it is like a demon wearing an angel's face. It lays low for a while only to slug us later, on the sly.[3]

Facing up to our sins, then, is the only healthful way to deal with them once and for all. We confess (admit) them to God. We repent, as Jesus asked the woman caught in adultery to do, turning from them and desiring to follow Him. We receive His grace and mercy thankfully, knowing we are loved, forgiven, and accepted. We make amends with anyone we've hurt. We file away in our minds the lessons we've learned, a little wiser and better prepared for the next temptation. And we move on.

## Moving On

As I've said before, I don't mean to suggest that this process is easy. Nor is it, in most cases, a do-it-once-and-you're-done situation. Especially at the emotional level, we may need to revisit some failures repeatedly before we find peace and healing. It is a process. Self-forgiveness may well be the hardest work we ever do.

In this area as in so many others, C.S. Lewis offers us a clear line of thinking: "There is no use in talking as if forgiveness were easy. We all know the old joke, 'You've given up smoking once; I've given it up a dozen times.' In the same way I could say of a certain man, 'Have I forgiven him for what he did that day? I've forgiven him more times than I can count.' For we find that the work of forgiveness has to be done over and over again."[4]

The same is true when it comes to forgiving ourselves. We may need to do it over and over, and that's OK. God has provided the means and the grace. He understands our emotions; He designed us and made us. He stands ready to help us.

God is and ever will be that loving Father pictured so beautifully in Luke 15, waiting eagerly for His prodigal children to turn once again toward home.

# twelve

# Learning to Bask in God's Grace

He makes just those who are unjust, forgives those who deserve to be punished, and favors those who deserve no favor.

CHARLES H. SPURGEON[1]

In the powerful motion picture *The Mission*, set in the South America of 1750, we are told the story of Captain Rodrigo Mendoza, a slave trader. Capturing the native Indians and selling them into bondage doesn't bother Mendoza's conscience; in fact, he seems proud of his ability to do his job well. But then one day, in a fit of anger over a woman they both love, Mendoza kills his brother Felipe.

That crime overwhelms Mendoza with guilt and remorse. Wanting to die, he goes to the local church and shuts himself off in a back room, refusing to eat. Finally, a priest named Father Gabriel comes to him and manages to engage him in a brief conversation.

"For me there is no redemption," Mendoza insists.

Eager to "pay" for killing his beloved brother, Mendoza accompanies Father Gabriel and his band of Jesuits back to their mission in the jungle, upriver from a spectacular waterfall hundreds of feet high. And as his penance, Mendoza drags behind him, everywhere he goes, a cargo net full of iron—armor, helmets, and the like. Each step he takes, even on level ground, requires enormous effort because the load he bears is so heavy.

In one of the film's most dramatic scenes, Mendoza ascends the waterfall still dragging his burden. Climbing enormous, spray-slicked boulders, the swinging weight of his load threatening to jerk him off the face of the cliff to certain death at any moment, he labors his way inch by inch to the top of the falls with steadfast determination.

Nothing will keep him from making the climb; nothing will keep him from carrying his burden with him.

As the journey continues, Mendoza and the party of priests reach a steep, wet hill that seems as if it must at last put an end to his efforts. He simply can't make it to the top, though every time he slips and falls back down the hill, he rises and tries again. Finally, in pity and frustration, one of the priests takes out his knife and cuts the rope binding Mendoza to his net full of iron.

The load goes rumbling and crashing to the bottom of the hill. Mendoza, watching it go, says nothing and shows no change from his stoic expression. When it smashes to a landing, he just walks down to it, ties it around his waist once again, and starts laboring back up the incline.

In his stubborn conviction that God will not forgive him, and that he could never forgive himself, Mendoza pictures so many of us Christians today. Whatever our sins, whether or not they're anywhere near as bad as Mendoza's, our feelings of guilt have led us to the ironclad conclusion that for us there is no redemption, or at least no lasting peace with God. We have tied ourselves to a burden, a sin-debt, that we will not let go.

## The Work Is Done

My prayer is that one result of this book will be a much greater sense of freedom and peace for those who read it, a willingness to let God remove the sin debt from us that His Son died to pay. The work of redemption is done; we have been made right with God by our trust in the death and resurrection of Jesus Christ on our behalf. Let's learn to bask in His grace.

We do not need to let the devil continue to make Rodrigo Mendozas of us.

In the imagery of the Bible, Jesus is pictured as both our High Priest and our sacrifice. The book of Hebrews, chapter 9, reminds us that under the Mosaic Law, Israel's high priest could enter the Holy of Holies in the tabernacle—the dwelling place of God on earth—only once a year, and then only if he carried a blood sacrifice for himself and the rest of the people. The work of Jesus, it goes on to say, was both similar and yet vitally different:

> For now Christ has come among us, the High Priest of the good things which were to come, and has passed through a greater and more perfect tent which no human hand had made (for it was no part of this world of ours). It was not with goats' or calves' blood but with his own blood that he entered *once and for all* into the holy place, *having won for us men [and women] eternal reconciliation with God.* For if the blood of bulls and goats and the ashes of a burnt heifer were, when sprinkled on the unholy, sufficient to make the body pure, then how much more will the blood of Christ himself, who in the eternal spirit offered himself to God as the perfect sacrifice, *purify our conscience from the deeds of death,* that we may serve the living God!
>
> HEBREWS 9:11-14, PHILLIPS, emphasis added

As that passage says, Jesus entered once and for all with the perfect sacrifice to satisfy God's justice. In doing so, He won for us *eternal* reconciliation with God. There is *nothing* left for us to do to be made right with God. Consequently, our consciences are clean—God holds nothing against us anymore. Everything we have ever done or will do wrong—every evil we've ever committed, every good thing we've failed to do—has been covered by the blood of Christ.

Think about that. Meditate on the passage again and again. Let its wonderful truth penetrate to the very marrow of your bones and to the deepest, most fear-filled recesses of your soul. *God loves you. God forgives you. God accepts you. Now and for all eternity, you are His and He is yours.*

Furthermore, because those things are true, the following are true of us as well:

We are God's children. (Jn 1:12)

We are God's friends. (Jn 15:15)

We have been justified, declared "not guilty" by God. (Rom 5:1)

We are united with the Lord and one with Him in Spirit. (1 Cor 6:17)

We have been bought with a price and so belong to God. (1 Cor 6:20)

We are members of Christ's body. (1 Cor 12:27)

We are saints, set apart as God's followers. (Eph 1:1)

We have direct access to God through the Holy Spirit. (Eph 2:18)

We are complete in Christ, lacking no spiritual resource
necessary to deal with our sin and guilt. (Col 2:10)

We are assured that all things work together for good.
(Rom 8:28)

We are free from any condemning charges against us. We
cannot be separated from the love of God. (Rom 8:31)

We have been established in our faith, anointed, and sealed
by God with His stamp of ownership. (2 Cor 1:21-22)

We are hidden with Christ in God. (Col 3:3)

We are citizens of heaven. (Phil 3:20)

We can find grace and mercy in time of need. (Heb 4:16)[2]

The list of incredible things that are ours because of being
in Christ could go on and on. But in the context of this book,
it all boils down to the simple fact that we are under God's
grace, not His condemnation, and we have no need to be burdened by a load of guilty feelings.

Let me encourage you, therefore, the next time and *every*
time you're feeling weighed down by guilt, to prayerfully
review the list above—the things that are ours *in Christ*. As
you read it, personalize it. For example, "*I* am God's child. *I*
am God's friend. *I* have been justified...." Take the time to
*thank* Him that each of those things is true. Ask Him by His
Spirit to press those truths deep into your soul. And ask Him
to transform you from guilt-ridden to joy-filled. He will!

### God's Not Finished

The next thing to keep in mind as we learn to bask in God's
grace is that while the work of reconciling us to Him is done,

He's not yet finished molding us into the image of His Son. We are works in progress. So we need to have the same patience with our shortcomings that God demonstrates daily.

The apostle Paul told us in the book of Romans, "For those God foreknew he also predestined to be conformed to the likeness of his Son, that he might be the firstborn among many brothers" (8:29). This process of making us more and more like Jesus began at the moment we placed our faith in Him and will continue for the rest of our lives. Sometimes we cooperate, and sometimes we don't. Regardless, God is committed to our spiritual growth.

In Philippians 1:6, Paul expressed the same truth this way: "Being confident of this, that he who began a good work in you will carry it on to completion until the day of Christ Jesus."

This patience with ourselves is, in fact, part of the Christlikeness that God is striving to develop in us. Galatians 5:22 tells us patience is part of the fruit the Holy Spirit wants to produce in us. Romans 5:3-4 explains that one reason we can rejoice in times of suffering is that they help produce patience, or perseverance, and character in us.

C.S. Lewis wrote of the process:

After each failure, ask forgiveness, pick yourself up, and try again. Very often what God first helps us towards is ... just this power of always trying again.... [T]his process trains us in habits of the soul.... It cures our illusions about ourselves and teaches us to depend on God. We learn, on the one hand, that we cannot trust ourselves even in our best moments, and, on the other, that we need not despair even in our worst, for our failures are forgiven.[3]

As God extends His grace and patience to us, so let us extend the same to ourselves.

## The Difference Love Makes

If this book leaves no other lasting impression, the one that I hope will endure is the fact that God loves us with a passionate, relentless, unshakable love. And the more we're able to grab hold of that truth—and let it grab hold of our hearts—the less we'll struggle with feeling guilty about things He has already forgiven.

Even apart from God, people realize the difference love makes. For instance, Will Smith, the actor and rap artist, said in appreciation of his parents' role in his life, "There's a certain level of confidence and self-esteem that comes from knowing for a fact that someone loves you."[4]

Now, as important to our well-being as parental love is, how much more confidence and self-esteem should we draw from knowing that the God of the universe loves us even more completely than a world-class mom and dad? Indeed, when the realization of the depth of God's love finally breaks through in a person's mind and heart, the effect can be nothing short of miraculous.

Jack Hall is a husband, father, and one-time pastor who got caught up in serious, habitual sin. His loving wife, Laurie, after learning of his addiction, hung on to hope through two years of counseling that ultimately proved fruitless.

At the end of that time, she asked for a separation. That was Jack's wake-up call to the fact that he had to change. But how? Where would he find the strength if professional counseling hadn't helped?

The answer didn't come quickly or easily. Months of searching and struggling went by. At last, a light began to dawn in the darkness of Jack's despair. Here's what it was, in Jack's own words:

The Lord gave me the courage to go through this tough process by showing me how much He loves me. I'd heard many times how much, but I never took it for myself. He gave me a vision of Christ on the cross, looking at me with tears in His eyes, saying: "Jack, I love you enough to die for you and you're not willing to receive that love. If you will, I will heal you of your past hurts so you can live free and I can finish that good work I've begun in you." ...

[W]hen I had that vision, I saw how my pride was spitting in the face of God's love and it broke me. He told me to stop doing and let Him heal me....

[H]ope came when I finally laid down my pride and began to accept that God loves me.[5]

As Max Lucado rightly observed, "God will not love you more if you're better tomorrow. God will not love you less if you're worse tomorrow. God's love does not ebb and flow or come and go."[6]

May we also, then, like Jack Hall, come to appreciate how great and unconditional a love our Father has for us and let Him heal us, starting with our unnecessary feelings of guilt. May we also, as we think and pray about the truths of God's Word that we've seen in this book, have a fresh, transforming vision of His grace. And when we do—when we make even the slightest turn in His direction or take even the smallest action that indicates our desire to draw nearer to Him—He will come running to embrace us, just like the prodigal's father in Luke 15.

### Freedom to Risk

Because we know we're works in progress and that God's love never fails, we're free to take risks in our Christian lives—to pursue our relationship with Him in ways that may not look exactly like those of the person in the next pew at church. If our desire is to please Him and to grow in our faith, we know our failures aren't final.

The legalists among us will tell us we must earn God's acceptance by doing a variety of things—having a daily devotional life, witnessing to others, living by a strict set of behavioral rules—and doing them their way. If we don't perform according to their standards or we lapse in some other way, they stand ready and eager to pile on the guilt.

What are some of the expectations of modern legalists? Many would say we're subpar Christians if we:

- don't school our children in a certain way (home school, Christian school, or public school, according to their personal bias).
- don't use a particular philosophy of discipline in rearing our kids.
- ever attend an R-rated movie.
- vote for the "wrong" political party.
- fail to have private devotions each and every day.
- go to a certain kind of church (again, according to their personal preference).
- aren't in church every time the doors are open.

The list could go on and on, but the point is that the free-dom-takers want to straitjacket our thinking and our choices, to confine our way of living for God to their narrowly defined range of what's right and wrong.

"For there to be true maturity," Chuck Swindoll wrote, "people must be given room to grow, which includes room to fail, to think on their own, to disagree, to make mistakes. Grace must be risked or we will be stunted Christians who don't think, who can't make decisions, who operate in fear and without joy because we know nothing but someone else's demands and expectations."[7]

But some will worry that if we're practicing this freedom to make our own decisions and even fail from time to time, liberty will give way to license. We'll be tempted to take advantage of God's grace and even stray into outright sin. What's to keep us from thinking we can do whatever we want, knowing we'll "get away with it"?

As we saw in chapter four, Romans 6 and 7 speak of our relationship with God through Jesus as the reason we seek to please Him rather than make light of His mercy. The apostle Paul, in 2 Corinthians 5:14-15, sums it up like this: "For Christ's love *compels* us, because we are convinced that one died for all, and therefore all died. And he died for all, that those who live should no longer live for themselves but for him who died for them and was raised again" (emphasis added).

That word *compels* in verse 14 is translated "controls" or "constrains" in other versions. The idea is that because of how greatly God has loved us, we are motivated to live for Him. That's the way, at the most basic level, we show that we love Him in return.

This is the antidote to license: not harsh, cold, legalistic rules, but living to please the lover of our souls.

Let's hope that we all have at least one other human being whom we love deeply—perhaps a mother, father, spouse, child, brother, or sister. How do we act with regard to that person? Do we intentionally do things that will hurt or disappoint her? Do we take advantage of his love and kindness to get what we want at his expense?

Because we're not perfect, the honest answer to both questions is sometimes yes. But for the most part, it's just the opposite. In fact, we go out of our way to please and satisfy the one we love. My wife, for example, is a loving, giving, hardworking person. Do I respond by putting her down or ignoring her needs? No, of course not. Though I blow it occasionally, my desire is to honor her and return her love. So I'm motivated to compliment her, to be grateful, to take her out to eat because I know she enjoys that, and to help her where I can.

Just so, our relationship as children of a loving, forgiving, accepting heavenly Father motivates us to please Him rather than try deliberately to hurt Him. We'll make mistakes; we'll fail; sometimes we'll lapse into taking Him for granted; but our basic desire will consistently be to honor Him and return His love.

Living with that as our goal is true freedom. Let's look again at Romans 6, this time focusing on verses 15-23 from the contemporary version known as *The Message*:

So, since we're out from under the old tyranny [having to obey the Mosaic Law], does that mean we can live any old way we want? Since we're free in the freedom of God, can we do anything that comes to mind? Hardly. You know well enough from your own experience that there are some acts of so-called freedom that destroy freedom. Offer yourselves to sin, for instance, and it's your last free act. But offer yourselves to the ways of God and the freedom never quits. All your lives you've let sin tell you what to do. But thank God you've started listening to a new master, one whose commands set you free to live openly in *his* freedom!

I'm using this freedom language because it's easy to picture. You can readily recall, can't you, how at one time the more you did just what you felt like doing—not caring about others, not caring about God—the worse your life became and the less freedom you had? And how much different is it now that you live in God's freedom, your lives healed and expansive in holiness?

As long as you did what you felt like doing, ignoring God, you didn't have to bother with right thinking or right living, or right *anything* for that matter. But do you call that a free life? What did you get out of it? Nothing you're proud of now. Where did it get you? A dead end.

But now that you've found you don't have to listen to sin tell you what to do, and have discovered the delight of listening to God telling you, what a surprise! A whole, healed, put-together life right now, with more and more of life on the way! Work hard for sin your whole life and your pension is death. But God's gift is *real life*, eternal life, delivered by Jesus, our Master.

That truth about what real freedom is, plus the patient love of God, leads us to live for Him.

## Faith, Not Feelings

As we learn to bask in God's grace, it can't be said often enough that we need to place our confidence, our trust, in the truths of God's Word, not in our feelings. Our emotions change easily and often, with regard to how guilty we are or aren't before Him as much as with anything else. *If we have confessed our sins to Him, we are forgiven.* Our guilt has been paid for and taken away forever.

That's the truth, and any suggestion to the contrary is a lie from the father of lies, reeking with the smoke of hellfire.

Indeed, one of the great tests of our Christian faith comes in those times of despair when our feelings tell us we've been deserted and condemned by the Almighty. Do we then turn our backs on Him and seek to make our own way in the world, or do we still trust Him and seek instead to do His will? Do we stumble or do we, in His strength, stand firm?

This was the test faced by the godly Job when his world fell apart around him. Things got so bad for him, with the loss of his children and possessions and the painful sores all over his own body, that his wife urged him, "Are you still holding on to your integrity? Curse God and die!" (Jb 2:9).

But Job, ultimately passing the test, declared, "Though he slay me, yet will I hope in him" (Jb 13:15).

Satan also recognizes the importance of such times of testing in our lives. C.S. Lewis captured that reality clearly in his classic book *The Screwtape Letters.* In one of the letters from Screwtape, a senior demon, to his protegé Wormwood, he wrote, "Do not be deceived, Wormwood. Our cause is never more in danger than when a human, no longer desiring, but still intending, to do our Enemy's [i.e., God's] will, looks round upon a universe from which every trace of Him seems to have vanished, and asks why he has been forsaken, *and still obeys*" (emphasis added).[8]

For that word *obeys*, we could also substitute *trusts, believes,* or *loves*. Because in such times—at all times—we have to decide for ourselves: Which is more true, more reliable, our feelings or God's Word?

## Helping Others

One of the benefits of our struggles with guilt—one of the goods that God can bring out of them—is the ability to help fellow strugglers with our hard-earned wisdom. "Praise be to the God and Father of our Lord Jesus Christ," Paul wrote, "the Father of compassion and the God of all comfort, who comforts us in all our troubles, so that we can comfort those in any trouble with the comfort we ourselves have received from God. For just as the sufferings of Christ flow over into our lives, so also through Christ our comfort overflows" (2 Cor 1:3-5).

By sharing what we've learned, we can become ministers of God's grace, setting others free from the bonds of legalism and unnecessary guilt, just as we have been freed. We can offer assurance of God's love, forgiveness, and acceptance to those burdened with fear and doubt. To those who, like the rest of us, battle with habitual sin, we can speak of God's provisions for growth and victory, and also of His understanding and patience.

In Matthew 5:14-16, Jesus said that we're to shine before the men and women of our world like warm lamps, drawing all those around us to our Father in heaven. When we serve Him as ministers of His grace, that is exactly what we'll be doing. I can think of no higher calling.

* * *

At the beginning of this book, I described guilt as a powerful emotion, one that seems to dominate the lives of many Christians. And I said that the only thing more powerful is the grace of God. That grace is, indeed, higher and wider and deeper than any other force in the universe, as vast as the One whose character it exemplifies.

It is stronger than Satan.

It is greater by far than our guilt.

It is exalted above our emotions and what they may tell us at any given moment.

It is, when all is said and done, the language of a divine love that simply will not let us go.

t h i r t e e n

# An Open Invitation

Are you tired? Worn out? Burned out on religion?
Come to me. Get away with me and you'll recover
your life. I'll show you how to take a real rest. Walk
with me and work with me—watch how I do it. Learn
the unforced rhythms of grace. I won't lay anything
heavy or ill-fitting on you. Keep company with me and
you'll learn to live freely and lightly.

JESUS, IN MATTHEW 11:28-30,
THE MESSAGE

Earlier in this book, I wrote of how I became a legalist in my formative years. For me at that time, the Christian life consisted mostly of a list of do's and don'ts—far more of the latter than of the former. I figured that if I was pretty much obedient to that list, I was pretty much a good Christian. But I was never entirely sure of how much God loved and accepted me.

The turnaround in my understanding began in a Bible study during my freshman year in college. As I looked into the Scriptures week by week, I gradually came to realize that God was more interested in my heart than in my behavior. He cared far more about how much I loved Him than He did about whether I ever played cards with a poker deck.

In other words, He cared immeasurably more about our relationship than He did about my adherence to any humanly devised set of rules.

I cannot tell you how freeing and exhilarating that revelation was! I felt as if my eyes had been opened and I had been handed the key to a set of shackles that had been locked tightly around my neck, wrists, and ankles. I felt free! And I began to develop a far greater appreciation than ever before of the love and grace God had extended to me in Jesus Christ.

If I can change the analogy, let me describe another way in which the experience affected me. I recently attended a men's retreat with my son at a Christian camp in the magnificent mountains of Colorado. We had never been there before and so we weren't familiar with the camp layout. And since we arrived after dark on a Friday evening, we couldn't see much beyond the faint glow of the occasional outdoor lamp.

Later that evening, we had to walk from our lodge to the meeting hall for the nightly assembly. As we approached the hall in the dark, I could tell that we were at the edge of the camp, that a big drop-off lay beyond the fence along the far side of the pathway. But I had no idea what was really out there. For all intents and purposes, it wasn't really there at all.

The next day, as I made that same walk in the morning light, an incredible scene opened before me.

Immediately in front as I approached the pathway, just to the left, were two brilliant golden aspen. Dropping down behind them was a valley sparkling in the early sun, on both sides a mix of dark green pines and more shining aspen. Beyond the valley stretched a broad plain dotted with ranch homes. And still farther beyond, as far as the eye could see from horizon to horizon, rising like a picture-postcard back-drop, stood a multilayered range of mountains. Peak upon peak, gray and distant, they loomed over all.

My years in legalism, if you will, were like viewing that scene in the darkness of night. The incredible beauty of God's grace was out there just in front of me. But because I couldn't see it, it might as well not have been.

Once the Holy Spirit began to open the eyes of my under-standing, however, it was like sitting on the edge of that valley as the sun rose with the dawn. Little by little, as the sun illumi-nated more and more of the fantastic scene, I was increasingly gripped with the wonder and majesty of the view. It was a sight to inspire painters and poets. I was amazed, over-whelmed. And I knew that I could keep looking for a lifetime and never see it all.

Up to the point that I began to more fully appreciate God's grace, I had thought I wanted to pursue the law as a vocation. A fitting occupation for a legalist, don't you think? But as I grew in my faith, I also felt a growing desire to help people more by introducing them to this same grace than by helping them with legal matters. (Understand, I still believe that lawyers can do a lot of good, but for me this was the right choice.) And so I have dedicated my professional life to editing and writing Christian books.

Over the years, I have developed gradually, in fits and starts, in my grasp on God's grace. As you've seen in these pages, my progress isn't always smooth, it continues to this day, and it will never conclude this side of heaven. Nonetheless, as I said in the very first chapter, there is now in the very core of my soul the absolute conviction that the grace of God is life's most powerful and profound truth. *And that realization has given me a quality of life, of relationship with Him, that no set of rules could ever come close to imitating.*

My prayer for you is that as you reflect on what you've read in these pages, meditate on the truths of God's Scriptures, and ask Him to open your own eyes, you, too, will come to appreciate the height and depth and breadth of His love and grace for you as never before. Perhaps you will grow in this understanding gradually, over a period of months and years. Or perhaps God will give you a sudden breakthrough, a revelation that immediately takes you to a new level of comprehension.

However it happens, my greatest hope is that in part because of the time you've spent with this book, you will one day (sooner rather than later, if it please God) be able join me in saying with assurance:

*I am loved by the God of the universe.*

*Because I have believed in Jesus Christ as my Lord and Savior, my sins are forgiven—every one of them: past, present, and future.*

*No matter what I have done in the past, no matter how bad, my guilt has been removed, and I am still fully loved and accepted by God.*

*Every time I sin,* regardless of how bad it is or even if it's the ten-thousandth time I've committed the same offense, *the heavenly Father is waiting to hear my confession and welcome me back into His gracious presence with open arms.*

*Absolutely nothing in this world, including my continuing struggles with sin, can ever separate me from God's love.*

Read those statements over and over. If it helps, write them out and put them in a place where you'll see them every day. Memorize the Bible verses listed in this book that back them up (see chapters two and ten), and let the Holy Spirit use His Word to transform your mind and your heart.

Is God good? Oh, yes. Does He love you? More than you'll ever know. But starting right now, you can know it more and more and forever.

## ONE
### *It Happened Years Ago*

1. Charles Swindoll, *The Grace Awakening* (Dallas: Word, 1990), 289.

## TWO
### *God's Truth About Our Guilt*

1. Paul Tournier, *Guilt and Grace* (New York: Harper & Row, 1962), 174.
2. David A. Seamands, *Healing Grace* (Wheaton, Ill.: Victor, 1988), 16.
3. C.S. Lewis, *Letters: C.S. Lewis/Don Giovanni Calabria*, trans. and ed. Martin Moynihan (Ann Arbor, Mich.: Servant, 1988), 67.

## THREE
### *When Our Feelings Get in the Way*

1. James Dobson, Focus on the Family broadcast, February 20, 1997.
2. Cheri Fuller and Louise Tucker Jones, *Extraordinary Kids* (Colorado Springs: Focus on the Family, 1997), 35.

3. James Dobson, *Emotions: Can You Trust Them?* (Ventura, Calif.: Regal, 1980), 9.
4. Quoted in *Plugged In,* Focus on the Family, August 15, 1997, 8.
5. Tournier, 39.
6. Lewis Smedes, *Forgive & Forget* (New York: Pocket, 1984), 98.
7. Tournier, 74-75.
8. Philip Yancey, *The Jesus I Never Knew* (Grand Rapids, Mich.: Zondervan, 1995), 37.
9. Tournier, 174.
10. Dobson, *Emotions: Can You Trust Them?*, 28-31.

FOUR

*Why Others Often Don't Help*

1. Seamands, 18.
2. Smedes, 102.
3. Tournier, 10.
4. Tournier, 12.

FIVE

*Our Struggle to Accept Unconditional Love*

1. A.W. Tozer, *Knowledge of the Holy* (San Francisco: Harper & Row, 1961), 9.
2. Henri Nouwen, *The Return of the Prodigal Son* (New York: Doubleday, 1992), 97.
3. Nouwen, 46.
4. Nouwen, 121.
5. Tournier, 189-90.
6. Tournier, 193.
7. Glenn Wagner, *The Heart of a Godly Man* (Chicago: Moody, 1997), chap. 3.

8. Quoted in John Eldredge, "The Thirst for God," *Aspire*, April-May 1997, 27.
9. Nouwen, 47.
10. C.S. Lewis, *Mere Christianity* (New York: Macmillan, 1943, 1945, 1952), 171-72.
11. C.S. Lewis, *Mere Christianity*, 174.
12. Max Lucado, *In the Grip of Grace* (Dallas: Word, 1996), 57-59.
13. Swindoll, *The Grace Awakening*, 63.
14. Stephen Brown, *If God Is in Charge* (Nashville: Nelson, 1983), 18.

## SIX
### *The Problem of Habitual Sin*

1. Lucado, 137.
2. Swindoll, *The Grace Awakening*, 22.

## SEVEN
### *The Lasting Consequences of Sin*

1. Tournier, 88.
2. Tournier, 140-41.
3. John Nieder and Thomas M. Thompson, *Forgive and Love Again* (Eugene, Ore.: Harvest House, 1991), 93, 104.

## EIGHT
### *Why a "Guilty" Christian May Be Satan's Favorite Kind*

1. Dobson, *Emotions: Can You Trust Them?*, 11.
2. Steve Shores, *False Guilt* (Colorado Springs, Colo.: NavPress, 1993), 7.
3. C.S. Lewis, *The Screwtape Letters* (New York: Macmillan, 1959), 132.

4. Quoted in Gregg A. Lewis, et al., *The Power of a Promise Kept* (Colorado Springs: Focus on the Family, 1995), 123-24.
5. Lucado, 145.


### NINE
#### *Gaining a Proper Perspective on God*

1. C.S. Lewis, *Letters of C. S. Lewis, 19 April 1951*, ed. W.H. Lewis (New York: Harcourt Brace Jovanovich, 1966), 230.
2. Swindoll, *The Grace Awakening*, 119.
3. Seamands, 23.
4. Swindoll, "Grace in a Barren Place," *New Man*, July-August 1997, 67.
5. Steve Thurman, "The Grace of God," a Fellowship Bible Church *Insight Paper* (Colo. Springs, n.d.).
6. Lucado, 145.


### TEN
#### *Trusting in God's Purposes*

1. Gregg A. Lewis, et al., 124.
2. Smedes, 97.
3. Tournier, 156-57.
4. Swindoll, *The Grace Awakening*, 71.
5. Gary Smalley, "Hidden Keys to Loving Relationships," video, Gary Smalley Seminars, Inc., 1994.
6. Swindoll, *The Grace Awakening*, 9.
7. C.S. Lewis, *Letters to an American Lady*, ed. Clyde Kilby (Grand Rapids, Mich.: Eerdmans, 1967), 77.

## ELEVEN
### *The Difference Between Forgiving and Forgetting*

1. Nieder and Thompson, 100.
2. Smedes, 61.
3. Smedes, 60.
4. C.S. Lewis, *Reflections on the Psalms* (New York: Harcourt, Brace & World, 1958), 24-25.

## TWELVE
### *Learning to Bask in God's Grace*

1. Charles H. Spurgeon, *All of Grace* (Grand Rapids, Mich.: Baker, 1976), 7.
2. Adapted from Neil T. Anderson, *Living Free in Christ* (Regal), in *New Man*, May 1997, 47.
3. C.S. Lewis, *Mere Christianity*, 93-94.
4. Quoted in *Plugged In*, Focus on the Family, September 15, 1997, 8.
5. "Ending an Affair of the Mind," an interview with Jack and Laurie Hall, *New Man*, May 1997, 40.
6. Max Lucado, speaking at the Denver Promise Keepers conference, June 22, 1996.
7. Swindoll, *The Grace Awakening*, 63.
8. C.S. Lewis, *The Screwtape Letters*, 39.

FEELING GUILTY

FINDING GRACE